WHEN
GOOD THINKING
GOES BAD

TODD C. RINIOLO

WHEN GOOD THINKING GOES BAD

How Your Brain Can Have a Mind of Its Own

Prometheus Books

59 John Glenn Drive
Amherst, New York 14228–2119

Published 2008 by Prometheus Books

Inquiries should be addressed to
Prometheus Books
59 John Glenn Drive
Amherst, New York 14228–2119
VOICE: 716–691–0133, ext. 210
FAX: 716–691–0137
WWW.PROMETHEUSBOOKS.COM

12 11 10 09 08   5 4 3 2 1

Library of Congress Cataloging-in-Publication Data

Riniolo, Todd C.
    When good thinking goes bad : how your brain can have a mind of its own / Todd C. Riniolo.
        p. cm.
    Includes bibliographical references and index.
    ISBN 978–1–59102–586–3
    1. Critical thinking. I. Title.

BF441.R56 2008
121'.6—dc22

2007038425

Printed in the United States of America on acid-free paper

To my children, with love

CONTENTS

ACKNOWLEDGMENTS

With a project such as this—the result of many years of research and teaching—it is unfortunately not possible to personally thank by name all those individuals who contributed in a variety of ways. Thus, sincere thanks to the many people who have generously and graciously given me their time, thoughts, and encouragement over the years. Likewise, thanks to those who challenged and forced me to rethink or refine my beliefs, as your contribution was invaluable.

I owe a great debt of gratitude to all those individuals whose work and scholarly endeavors have influenced and contributed to this book. Once again, the list is far too long to name everyone, but certain individuals should be recognized. Thus, thanks to skeptics James Randi, Michael Shermer, Martin Gardner, and Harry Houdini; philosophers Sidney Hook and Paul Kurtz; economists Thomas Sowell, F. A. Hayek, Julian Simon, and Milton Friedman; psychologists Thomas Gilovich, Ray Hyman, Elizabeth Loftus, David Myers, and Michael Mahoney; journalist John Stossel; and last, but certainly not least, Charles Darwin.

Special thanks to my colleagues Lee Nisbet and Jerry Erion,

whose willingness to provide feedback and discuss a wide range of issues greatly benefited the conception and ultimately the final version of this book. In addition, I would like to thank everyone at Prometheus Books, especially Steven L. Mitchell and Lynette Nisbet, for their editorial feedback and encouragement and for making this process an enjoyable one for the author.

Also, I would like to thank Howard Reid, who first sparked my interest in critical thinking in an undergraduate research methods course at Buffalo State College. Likewise, special thanks to Stephen Porges, Olga Bazhenova, and Jane Doussard-Roosevelt, who provided mentorship in research methods during my graduate school years at the University of Maryland that everyone should be lucky enough to experience.

My closest friends (Mike Augello, Chuck Bender, Lou Schmidt, Joe Schwartz) always provided an open forum for me to share my ideas. Of course, many thanks to my wife, Angela, my kids, Kate and Thomas, and the rest of my family, who make life much more enjoyable than it would otherwise be, and whose patience with me when working on projects such as this is often above and beyond the call of duty. Note that the usual disclaimers apply, as none of the above-mentioned individuals should be held responsible for the views that are ultimately the responsibility of the author.

Finally, I'd like to thank the reader for taking the time to consider the arguments presented in this book.

INTRODUCTION

Every man, wherever he goes, is encompassed by a cloud of comforting con-victions, which move with him like flies on a summer day.
                    —Bertrand Russell, *Skeptical Essays* (1938, p. 28)

If you're like me, you love reading skeptical books (e.g., *Flim-Flam, Why People Believe Weird Things*) and articles from skeptical publications (e.g., *Skeptic, Skeptical Inquirer*) that emphasize the importance of critical thinking, especially when the critical thinker demolishes some widely held, foolish belief that is accepted as fact by many non-critical thinkers (e.g., the "curse of King Tut," the accuracy of Nostradamus's predictions, the effectiveness of distant prayers healing the sick). I must admit that I root for the critical thinkers, as I identify with them and consider myself to be part of a community of individuals that share my conviction in the benefits of critical thinking and rigorously evaluating evidence. Knowing that there are other people like me is comforting, especially when I am the only person at a social or family gathering who does not believe in such things as "psychic powers" or who does not uncritically accept some trendy new belief.

As a college professor, I have found that using critical thinking to evaluate paranormal claims is a very effective way to generate and maintain student interest, even in those students whose eyes typically start to glaze over once the topics "critical thinking" or "research methods" are even hinted at in the classroom. I regularly teach a course on skepticism and the paranormal as a way to keep student motivation high in an area that I am passionate about, the application of research methods to evaluate evidence. I consider myself to be both a critical thinker (the reader may disagree by the end of this book!) and an advocate of critical thinking, as critical thinking is ultimately the best way to evaluate evidence and develop an informed opinion or belief.

Yet, one important question for us as critical thinkers to consider that has not received adequate attention but may have important implications is the following: Are we, as critical thinkers who have the knowledge, skills, and experience to successfully implement our critical thinking skills, also on occasion vulnerable to uncritically accepting important information? Potentially even worse, are we from time to time vulnerable to believing in silly things even on important issues? This book is an attempt to think about and explain why everyone is prone in certain instances to go astray (i.e., to either be inconsistent with the application of critical thinking or to abandon it altogether). If this assertion is correct (the rationale and supporting evidence is provided in part II), and nobody is immune from thinking uncritically in some contexts, then raising this issue can have some very positive benefits for us as critical thinkers in the long run and can ultimately be useful to improve the application of our individual critical thinking skills in a more consistent manner and to a wider range of issues. For example, an active awareness that we have the potential to go astray can increase our due diligence as critical thinkers, can help to prevent or minimize overconfidence in our beliefs that have not been subjected to rigorous scrutiny, and can ultimately be used to identify those specific instances in which each of us is most likely to go off track.

As a personally embarrassing example, I once actually took a Hollywood movie at face value as an accurate reflection of an important historical event (see chapter 9 for further details), despite the fact that I am well educated and typically do not rely upon secondhand sources for important information (see chapter 4), a concept that I repeatedly stress when teaching. In this instance (and likely others), I did not practice what I preach, and it was surprisingly easy for me to unknowingly abandon the standards of critical thinking that I am well aware of and typically implement. This book will ultimately theorize that our own beliefs, especially our most cherished beliefs, can in certain situations influence our ability to appropriately apply our critical thinking skills that usually serve us well. In essence, we are all inconsistent critical thinkers. Even the elite critical thinker is not exempt. I am hoping that the reader who is skeptical of my claim at this point will give me the opportunity to make the case, as the ultimate goal of this book is to sharpen the skills of the critical thinker by increasing awareness that we are all, in select instances, vulnerable to uncritical thinking. If my assertion does not stand up to critical scrutiny, then no real harm besides some wasted time has been done by considering the argument. The emphasis of this introduction is to discuss this issue in a little more detail and frame the discussion for the remainder of the book.

CRITICAL THINKING FOR EVALUATING CLAIMS

Various terms have been used to define critical thinking by a wide range of authors, and critical thinking encompasses a variety of domains (e.g., reasoning, decision making, problem solving). Here, in order to keep the discussion manageable, let's focus on some pertinent aspects of critical thinking as it relates specifically to the evaluation of claims (e.g., does the person have psychic abilities?). When we talk about the appropriate application of critical thinking to evaluate specific claims, two widely agreed-upon key components are the *attitude toward the claim* and the *method of inquiry*. First, at the heart of critical thinking is the belief that claims should be evaluated. When a person claims to have psychic powers, the ability to speak with the dead, or the ability to cure cancer with divine powers, critical thinking does not blindly accept the claim at face value but responds with "OK, let's see your best evidence." Thus, critical thinking requires an evidence-demanding attitude or mind-set that actively seeks information as opposed to passively receiving input. Moreover, critical thinking has a "nothing is off-limits" policy. Thus, not even our most precious beliefs are exempt from a critical evaluation.

Second, the appropriate application of critical thinking to evaluate claims not only demands evidence but will subsequently require that the specific evidence is gathered and rigorously evaluated by implementing the scientific method, which is the process of inquiry that is required. Simply put, not all evidence is equal. For example, nonscientific evidence, such as thirdhand stories about the effectiveness of a "psychic" treatment for depression, is not given the same weight as evidence that is obtained and evaluated using scientific procedures, such as a rigorous, randomized double-blind study. When we talk about the scientific method, it is important to keep in mind that the scientific method does not have a one-size-fits-all approach for evaluating all claims (i.e., different claims can require different scientific approaches). Thus, a critical evaluation of a potentially haunted hotel may use different methods of inquiry than those used to test an individual for extrasensory abilities, to evaluate the effectiveness of an alternative treatment for cancer, or to test the Shroud of Turin for authenticity. The common threads of critical thinking related to the evaluation of claims is once again this evidence-demanding attitude and the use of scientific methods, which can vary depending upon the specific claim being evaluated. (The reader may have noticed that critical thinking for the evaluation of claims is consistent with skepticism. Thus, I may at times use the term *skepticism* when referring to how critical thinking evaluates claims, and *skeptic* when referring to the critical thinker.)

While applying critical thinking to various claims does not always lead the individual to the correct conclusion (no method of inquiry is 100 percent accurate in ascertaining the truth), it does increase the chances of making an informed evaluation. Thus, skepticism provides us with information to help guide judgments and decisions. For example, imagine the disadvantage you would be at if you had an uncritical mind-set when purchasing a used car and simply relied upon the salesperson's assurances that you were getting a "great deal."

Beliefs that are the result of objectively applying our critical thinking skills have a greater probability of approximating the truth than those that have not been rigorously evaluated but simply accepted at face value. Furthermore, the critical evaluation of claims should not simply be thought of as a "debunking" technique that only seeks to discredit, but rather a method that can gather and evaluate evidence that is favorable, ambiguous, or unfavorable to the specific claim (i.e., the car could be a great deal).

In addition, critical thinking is not an ideological position (i.e., it has no vested interests in the outcome of any claim) but is only loyal to ascertaining the truth. Thus, the critical thinker should be objective, suspend judgment, and be an unbiased evaluator of claims swayed by evidence because the scientific method requires those standards. Likewise, critical thinking does not root for a particular outcome and has no tolerance for anyone that purposely misleads or presents evidence in a biased manner. Ideally, a critical investigation should be both an empirical and objective evaluation of a claim, such as investigating whether or not individuals who rely upon intuitive judgments actually have successful outcomes. If intuition is an effective strategy, great! If intuition fails miserably, great! For those interested in what circumstances and what types of individuals intuition is likely to succeed or fail, see *Intuition* (Myers 2002), which summarizes this interesting concept.

THE DIFFERENCE BETWEEN ABILITY AND PERFORMANCE

One of the important themes to keep in mind as you make your way through this book is the distinction between our ability as critical thinkers and our performance as critical thinkers (this would apply to all the domains covered by critical thinking, but once again, let's focus specifically on evaluating claims). Taking the information provided above, let's assume that an individual critical thinker possesses the ability to maintain the standards (e.g., demands evidence, objectively and rigorously evaluates) and implement the procedures (e.g., scientific inquiry) that are used to evaluate claims. While ability often matches or closely approximates performance leading to a successful evaluation of a claim (here success is defined as demanding evidence and objectively and rigorously applying scientific methods), performance can also deviate from ability in certain situations. While this distinction between ability and performance seems obvious, it has potentially important implications for us to consider.

As an analogy, the critical thinker can be viewed like a professional baseball player playing the field (keep in mind that all of us have varying skill levels; I am more like a "sandlot" baseball player). Here, the critical thinker possesses the ability to successfully field ground balls and in most instances achieves that goal (i.e., a successful outcome). However, once the ball is hit by the batter, the baseball player actually has to perform and carry out the task of fielding the ball. Thus, there exists the possibility that the player will not appropriately use his ability (i.e., deviate from his training and skill level) and make an error under certain conditions (i.e., performance does not match ability). Likewise, there exists the possibility we may slip up and not use our critical thinking ability appropriately when evaluating all important claims. Thus, both the baseball player and the critical thinker must have due diligence and not develop an overconfidence and automatically assume the task will be successfully completed, even though each possesses the necessary ability to do so.

As one example, skeptics of paranormal claims (e.g., James Randi, Michael Shermer, Paul Kurtz) have correctly pointed out that the media is biased toward the paranormal and have cautioned believers in psychic phenomena against uncritical acceptance of media reports. I wholeheartedly agree with this warning, and countless examples could be given to support this assertion. Yet, I would wager, despite the fact that we are all aware that the media can misrepresent issues to make a more compelling story, all of us have at one time or another uncritically accepted media reports on issues for which we already possess strong beliefs, such as economic, medical, political, social, and/or environmental claims. This most often occurs when the information presented by the media is consistent with our preexisting beliefs. In those situations, we may not appropriately apply our critical thinking and demand and rigorously evaluate evidence, just like the baseball player who takes his eyes off the ball and makes an error. Unfortunately, as we all are aware and have seen many examples of in the noncritical thinker, uncritical acceptance of important information is the first step toward developing a silly belief.

SKEPTICAL OF THE CRITICAL THINKER AS INCONSISTENT

Of course, many readers are likely questioning my description of all critical thinkers (even elite critical thinkers) as having the potential to uncritically accept information on important issues and will demand evidence to support the theory that we as critical thinkers can inconsistently apply our skills (or may abandon them altogether) when evaluating claims under certain conditions. While the theory will be elaborated upon and evidence presented later in the book (see part II), the idea is based upon the simple notion that we are all human and are influenced by our evolutionary heritage (which we are often unaware of). Specifically, one aspect of our evolutionary heritage that psychologists have been documenting for years is a variety of cognitive biases that influence our ability to accurately and consistently evaluate claims (our biased cognitive systems will be discussed in chapter 7). Psychologist Thomas Gilovich (1993, 50) nicely articulates one example, "When examining evidence relevant to a given belief, people are inclined to see what they expect to see, and conclude what they expect to conclude. Information that is consistent with our pre-existing beliefs is often accepted at face value, whereas evidence that contradicts them is critically scrutinized and discounted. Our beliefs may thus be less responsive than they should to the implications of new information." While we as critical thinkers can control the influence of preexisting beliefs for some evaluations (this takes due diligence), in other contexts we may be unaware that our beliefs are interfering with our ability to think critically. Thus, our performance may suffer.

Likewise, *humans are biased toward strengthening and maintaining our current beliefs (both true and false).* These biases have the potential to influence whether or not we pursue a skeptical investigation of a claim, can interfere with our ability to objectively evaluate evidence, and can inhibit our ability to modify our beliefs in response to new evidence (see chapter 7). It is a fundamental flaw to assume that the mind is not influenced by the process of natural selection and that critical thinking skills exempt us from the biases that are part of our evolutionary heritage. Interestingly, research has demonstrated that scientists are not immune from the same biases that everyone else possesses, despite training to implement the scientific method in an objective and unbiased manner (see chapters 7 and 8). The good news is that developing an active awareness that we are influenced by cognitive biases can allow us to implement strategies to counteract our biased nature (or field the difficult ground ball).

As a personal example of how beliefs can influence the application of critical thinking, my current views about the effectiveness of alternative medicine are extremely negative (i.e., I consider it nothing more than quackery). Thus, when a claim is made that beestings can help people with arthritis, I typically dismiss the claim out of hand (perhaps some claims do have merit) or if I have the time will search out the evidence, such as published studies, and evaluate the evidence critically, looking for flaws in the research design and simpler explanations of results (e.g., placebo effect; see chapter 3). However, I do not routinely do this when a new type of surgery makes a similar claim (I have a very positive view toward modern Western medicine, which is typically justified based upon its many successes). Thus, the information is uncritically accepted, and my current belief in Western medicine is reinforced without the benefit of a skeptical inquiry into the specific claim.

However, just like the beestings or a host of other alternative medical treatments, some types of surgery have not been demonstrated to be any more effective than a comparable placebo under double-blind conditions. As an example, in patients with knee arthritis, "fake" surgery (i.e., a placebo condition) was just as effective as arthroscopic surgery in providing pain relief (Moseley, O'Malley, Petersen, Menke, et al. 2002). Thus, a clear double standard (i.e., inconsistent critical thinking) occurs. I should apply the evidence demanding attitude and rigorous evaluation to both claims (especially if I were considering the treatments for a medical condition) but typically do not, just as the large literature within cognitive psychology predicts. My preconceived views can ultimately influence my critical thinking performance. Furthermore, awareness that I am prone to uncritically accepting information that is consistent with my overall belief in the effectiveness of modern Western medicine (once again, usually justified based upon the many successes) can be useful to ensure that I critically evaluate specific claims and minimize inconsistent critical thinking.

THE ORIGINS OF OUR BELIEFS

In order to understand why everyone is vulnerable in certain contexts to uncritically accept information (that can ultimately lead to a silly belief), let's discuss the origins of our beliefs; because what we currently believe biases us in a variety of ways (see chapters 7 and 9). Unfortunately, none of us (not even the author, a college professor with plenty of free time!) has the time or the adequate expertise to apply critical thinking to the evaluation of every potential claim. Thus, many of our beliefs have developed independent of the skeptical process, which decreases the likelihood of a correct evaluation. (As a quick side issue, I am not advocating a universal skepticism, which is being critical and demanding evidence of every claim. Universal skepticism eventually becomes self-defeating, and simple time restraints require all of us to accept some information without critical scrutiny. However, I am arguing that our current beliefs do influence how we evaluate even some important claims.)

Specifically, everyone takes shortcuts and uses strategies, such as relying upon what is commonly believed (e.g., Freud discovered the unconscious, which is false), relying upon experts (e.g., exercise is beneficial for long-term health, which appears true based upon the current evidence; however, experts are not always correct), relying upon information obtained from media reports (e.g., newspaper articles, press releases, radio, television, Internet; see chapter 4 for further discussion of media reporting), relying upon what colleagues or friends have told us, identifying patterns based primarily on personal experience, and so on. In these cases, we are not practicing critical thinking but taking a shortcut for practical reasons, just like the noncritical thinker. Relying upon shortcuts when making decisions and/or evaluations is common and necessary (see Cialdini 2001), but it does put us in a vulnerable position and increases the likelihood that we have accepted false beliefs, even on important issues, compared with those beliefs that have been subjected to an objective and rigorous evaluation.

Some of our beliefs are already formed and reinforced prior to learning how to think critically and demand evidence (e.g., being told as a child that you would catch a cold in the winter if you did not wear a warm jacket). Also, some beliefs are formed based primarily upon an emotional evaluation (e.g., a parent evaluating their child's talents, lovers accurately evaluating their partner's personality characteristics). Simply put, we all have many beliefs that have not been subjected to an appropriate critical inquiry for a variety of reasons. (Of course, I would argue that the critical thinker has fewer false beliefs compared with the gullible believer.) Nonetheless, *all of our current beliefs, both true and false, ultimately influence our critical thinking performance.*

An awareness of the origins of our beliefs is vital because we all have the very human tendency to have great confidence in all of our beliefs and lose track of how the beliefs originated. A simple question to ask ourselves is: Is that particular belief the result of a rigorous and objective investigation? The critical thinker who does not ask himself that basic question is at a substantial disadvantage compared to those who actively evaluate the origins of their personal beliefs. We should not have as much confidence in individual beliefs that have not been thoroughly evaluated, as opposed to those that have gone through the rigorous process of a critical evaluation (a theme emphasized in this book).

For example, I personally advocate a low-fat/high-carbohydrate diet as the healthiest lifestyle choice. Tracing the origins of that belief, it is primarily composed of antidotal information, some personal experience and personal preference, some isolated media reporting, and virtually no critical analysis of any firsthand information. Likewise, nutrition is not an area in which I have taken any time to gain any specific expertise. Thus, I have not become familiar with or critically analyzed evidence, but I have relied upon shortcuts to construct my belief. Yet, ask me what I recommend people eat, and I'll tell you low-fat/high-carbs, but the belief is based upon very flimsy evidence. I could be correct, but I should not have as much confidence in that belief as I do in others that I have taken the time to subject to rigorous scrutiny.

In contrast, I feel very confident telling the reader that thermally stressful conditions, such as hot and humid environments, can influence cognitive development in humans (see Riniolo and Schmidt 2006 for the theoretical rationale and supporting evidence). However, that belief is based upon a critical inquiry and has withstood peer review, and the scientific evidence that could be listed to support the belief is substantial and has been critically evaluated. There is a difference in the origins and quality of the evidence that supports the beliefs (and here in the expertise I currently possess in those specific areas). Thus, the confidence that I should have in the two beliefs should be different, and an awareness of the difference in the quality of the evidence to support the beliefs is essential for us as critical thinkers, as nobody's entire belief system has been subjected to critical scrutiny. Imagine how foolish I could appear if I publicly presented my views on a topic in which I lack even a basic competence and the beliefs were supported by such flimsy evidence as personal preference and my own limited experience. (As a side note, I still think I'm correct about low-fat/high-carbs! It can be difficult to shake the high confidence we have in our beliefs even if they are supported by minimal evidence.)

AN EXAMPLE FROM THE CLASSROOM

When teaching my skeptics course to undergraduate students, I typically start the semester by stressing the importance of the evidence-demanding attitude and will subsequently provide opportunities for students to develop and practice their skills for the appropriate evaluation of paranormal and pseudoscientific claims. It is gratifying to observe students increase their ability to think critically and to use their new research skills to evaluate claims. However, I also believe it is important for students to gain experience that shows them that despite their ability to think critically, they should not automatically assume they will now think critically in all instances (i.e., performance may not match ability). With that in mind, I was interested to see how students would perform once the context was changed. I started the class off with the following question, which I now routinely use as a teaching tool: "Should the minimum wage be raised in the United States?"

Note that this question is not within the realm of the supernatural (my students had demonstrated proficiency in critical thinking in this context), but it is an important issue within the realm of economics that could impact many individuals in a variety of ways (the purpose of this exercise was not to provide a definitive answer but to evaluate if students would implement their critical thinking skills by demanding and seeking out evidence to evaluate the claim). I chose this question because many individuals have very strong opinions when it comes to economic issues and claims (i.e., preexisting beliefs), likely because we all have a variety of personal experiences to draw upon. For example, like many of my students, I personally have had several "crappy" minimum-wage jobs when I was younger (one was a graveyard-shift job in a factory during the summer) and would have loved to have been paid more (i.e., a worker's perspective). In contrast, others have such experiences as helping to run a family business and would be concerned with keeping salaries at a certain level (i.e., an owner's perspective).

In any case, the same students who asked critical questions, demanded evidence, sought out empirical studies, looked for and critically evaluated expert opinion, and so on when it came to paranormal issues, now abandoned the skeptical approach when it came to the minimum wage question. In fact, knee-jerk responses were typical and confidence in their opinions very high. However, the opinions (both for and against) were supported primarily by limited personal experience, an emotional response, or what was presented in the media on this topic. My students were well aware that personal experience, emotional responses, and media presentations are typically the "evidence" given for beliefs in paranormal claims!

An important aspect of this exercise was that it ultimately stressed to students the importance of identifying when they have not performed a critical inquiry and when they have inadequate information to provide an informed opinion (once again, the goal here was not to provide a concrete answer but to reinforce that critical thinking demands the evidence-seeking attitude, not the knee-jerk response). Thus, an awareness of our lack of knowledge on a specific topic is an important aspect of critical thinking because there exists a difference in the quality of those beliefs that have been rigorously evaluated and those that have not. The positive aspect of this exercise was that students were less likely to have the knee-jerk response when the context was changed in subsequent exercises.

For those who will be teaching courses in critical thinking, here are a few other questions that can reinforce the above lesson: Are teachers underpaid? Is there a "greatest" generation? What is the likelihood that someone getting married this year will get divorced (you may wish to find out how the 50 percent statistic used in media reports is actually calculated)? Are women paid less than men for equal work? Does talk therapy have any benefit for patients beyond a simple placebo effect? Do we have more, less, or the same amount of free time as previous generations? Is multiple personality disorder (MPD) a legitimate diagnosis, or is MPD a socially constructed phenomenon? Do computers increase overall student learning? It is interesting to ask students how many of them have simply accepted, without any critical inquiry, the common beliefs on these issues. Sometimes common beliefs are correct, sometimes they are not. A critical inquiry is the method that provides the best vehicle to differentiate between the two.

AN EXAMPLE OF AN OUTSTANDING INCONSISTENT CRITICAL THINKER

Since this book is putting forth the claim that we are all vulnerable to inconsistently applying our critical thinking under certain conditions, I believe it is important to provide the reader with a concrete example of an exceptional skeptic who rigorously applied critical thinking to a large number of claims, but who in isolated instances was prone to uncritically accepting information. Isaac Asimov (the purpose here is not to attack Asimov personally, but to illustrate the point that everyone, even an outstanding critical thinker and someone as brilliant as Asimov, is influenced by our evolutionary heritage), who was ranked as the sixth most outstanding skeptic of the twentieth century by the fellows and scientific consultants of the Committee for the Scientific Investigation of Claims of the Paranormal (CSICOP; now called the Committee for Skeptical Inquiry), was an outstanding critical thinker. As the *Skeptical Inquirer* (2000, 24:26) correctly notes, Asimov "loved the historical approach. . . . Asimov was a steadfast defender of science and reason and foe of nonsense, superstition, and pseudoscience." I agree with this interpretation, and there is no doubt that Asimov was an elite critical thinker. Yet, like all of us, his personal beliefs influenced his critical thinking performance.

Specifically, Asimov uncritically accepted and endorsed one of the "doomsday" predictions that were trendy in the late 1960s and early 1970s. Asimov signed his name (and reputation) to a full-page advertisement sponsored by the Environmental Fund that appeared in leading newspapers (such as the *Wall Street Journal*) in 1975, which said the following (cited in Simon 1981, 55):

> The world as we know it will likely be ruined before the year 2000 and the reason for this will be its inhabitants' failure to comprehend two facts. These facts are:
>
> 1. World food production cannot keep pace with the galloping growth of population.

2. "Family planning" cannot and will not, in the foreseeable future, check this runaway growth.

The predication endorsed by Asimov was flat-out wrong and seems almost humorous today, given that obesity is a more pressing issue, some countries pay farmers not to grow food, food is currently being used for fuel (my gas at the pump contains 10 percent ethanol), and some countries are concerned about underpopulation. This is not to imply that all individuals had enough to eat during this time, but lack of food was not due to lack of world food production (some scientists at the time were even recommending that those who did need help should be allowed to starve to death because of the "overpopulation" threat). From a historical perspective, which Asimov brilliantly applied to the evaluation of a large number of other types of claims, there have been *numerous* of these types of doomsday population/starvation predictions (like the religious apocalyptic predictions; see Randi 1997) that have all come and gone (i.e., were wrong) starting with Malthus in 1798. During the 1970s, many similar "end of the world as we know it" predictions were common. The critical thinker should have been skeptical about the accuracy of the current prediction based upon the accuracy of all of the past predictions and demanded evidence to support the above "facts." As critical thinkers, we all are skeptical of any future psychic prediction based upon the miserable record of previous psychic predictions. Yet, Asimov signed his name to that prediction, and he should be evaluated accordingly.

So, what was the actual evidence that supported the dire prediction? The consensus among agricultural economists (i.e., experts in world food production) at the time was not consistent with the prediction of mass starvations but that improvements in world food supplies were occurring (Simon 1981). The only data available on this issue at the time (from either the US Department of Agriculture or the United Nations Food and Agriculture Organization) flatly contradicted the notion that food production could not keep pace with population growth (it was increasing and continued to improve until the end of the century!). In order for an individual to believe the prediction that the world was going to "likely be ruined" in the next twenty-five years, either there was no evidence seeking or the best available evidence was ignored without providing a compelling justification. Thus, the prediction was supported by a speculative statement (not a "fact") that was in direct contrast to the best available evidence at the time, and historically similar predictions had a miserable performance record.

Likewise, these types of population/starvation predictions have historically made questionable assumptions about humans that must be accepted in order to support the beliefs. These supporting assumptions should also be critically evaluated, for example, the assumption that no technological advances will occur in the future (a strange assumption in an age of science, particularly from a writer of science fiction) and that humans do not change their reproductive behavior in response to changing circumstances (humans are assumed to behave like flies reproducing in a jar; these points will be addressed in further detail in chapter 13). Empirical evidence and human history are inconsistent with both of these assumptions.

Of course, Asimov is not alone, as all critical thinkers in varying contexts (depending upon their individual beliefs), are vulnerable to believe in some nonsense if they uncritically accept information without due diligence. The author is not excluding himself, and he is sure the reader will find some examples of his fallibility in this book! Finally, Asimov was chosen as an example because he was such a brilliant critical thinker, and in most contexts he was a shining example of what we should all strive to emulate. In fact, I would argue that if he had applied his normal critical thinking skills to the speculative claim he ultimately publicly endorsed as a fact, he would have come to a different conclusion. Here, however, he can serve as an example to the rest of us that nobody is immune (not even the elite critical thinker) from uncritically accepting important information.

WHO SHOULD READ THIS BOOK?

First, this book is meant for any individual who is interested in critical thinking. It is meant for a general audience. I have tried to keep the technical language to a minimum and I provide examples when possible to illustrate key points that are supported by empirical evidence. Second, this book is also intended for college professors who are interested in putting together a course in critical thinking/skepticism, or as a potential supplemental book for students. Unlike in most other books, skepticism here is applied (the reader can judge how well) to a wide variety of claims beyond just the typical paranormal and pseudoscientific examples to help stress the ability/performance distinction. In contrast to this introduction, I have attempted to alert the reader to what I consider useful resources on the topics covered in this book. However, I wish to apologize in advance, as some areas of the book may have too many citations and others too few. I tried, but perhaps failed, in keeping a reasonable balance. If I have failed to provide the reader with an important reference, you can feel free to contact me at todd.c.riniolo@medaille.edu, and I will do my best to provide the supporting documentation. Also, for those reading the book with a limited background in critical thinking, I would recommend reading the book in order for appropriate context, whereas other readers may wish to jump around at their leisure.

Of course, this book is also meant for the critical thinker. As previously mentioned, the distinction between ability and performance is an important one to continually remind ourselves of, and it can ultimately result in increasing our performance as critical thinkers if we are vigilant and can identify those situations in which we have the potential to become inconsistent or abandon our critical thinking altogether. In addition, this book is intended to challenge the critical thinker to determine what personal beliefs (particularly strongly held ones) have been generated via a rigorous evaluation, and which beliefs have simply come about via alternative means. This may be particularly important when we wander outside of our individual field of expertise (i.e., like the baseball player having to field a new position) without familiarizing ourselves with the basics of the discipline.

FORMAT OF THE BOOK

With that background information in mind, the format of this book is relatively straightforward. Part I will provide the reader with some of the hallmarks of critical thinking as it relates to the evaluation of claims. This section is not meant to be exhaustive but should provide the reader who is attempting to learn about critical inquiry with some of the basics. Specific topics to be covered include critical thinking in everyday life, the questions critical thinkers ask, the role of experts in evaluating claims, double-blind procedures, the placebo effect, the law of parsimony, why strange coincidences are normal, and why we should be skeptical of secondhand sources, such as media reports. This section will rely primarily upon paranormal and pseudoscientific claims to provide examples. In addition, part I will demonstrate the inconsistency of applying some of the hallmarks of critical thinking to various claims in part III.

Part II of the book, using an evolutionary framework, will address several important issues related to why we may be inconsistent with our critical thinking in certain contexts. In addition, this section will review the cognitive literature that indicates that once beliefs are formed, we have built-in cognitive biases that can interfere with our ability to seek out contradictory evidence, accurately evaluate claims, and modify our beliefs when new evidence is presented. While the focus of this book is on the cognitive biases, the role of emotions will also be addressed. Finally, this section will use case examples of an ordinary critical thinker (myself) and a brilliant mind to illustrate that nobody is immune from our evolutionary heritage.

Part III will focus on specific examples by using a wide range of claims across various disciplines in an attempt to illustrate how everyone is potentially vulnerable to inconsistently applying their critical thinking skills in certain contexts. This portion of the book will focus not on increasing our critical thinking skills (which is important, but is covered in detail by many other authors) but on using the abilities we already possess in a more consistent manner across a wider range of claims. For example, the same standards used by the critical thinker when investigating a psychic claim will be applied to the global warming debate. Likewise, political and multicultural claims will also be investigated, as well as a comparison between skeptics and economists. I will even attempt to defend Santa Claus, as some have used highly speculative arguments trying to link old Saint Nick with a lack of critical thinking in today's society. Preposterous! The examples used were chosen because (a) many individuals have strong preexisting beliefs on these types of topics, which can ultimately influence our critical thinking performance, and (b) a critical evaluation leads to different conclusions on these issues than does the conventional wisdom (the reader is encouraged to challenge this assertion by conducting her own critical inquiry).

In short, the later chapters of the book are designed to provide examples of potential inconsistent critical thinking by branching out well beyond the paranormal, as it is a challenge to maintain our critical thinking across a variety of contexts because of the influence of our preexisting beliefs. Of course, the author himself is not immune, and expects to hear from the reader when his inconsistencies are identified. Hopefully the reader will not find an instance when I have abandoned the critical approach altogether! Finally, the conclusion will contain some brief parting thoughts.

Part I

SOME HALLMARKS OF CRITICALLY EVALUATING CLAIMS

The purpose of part I is to give the reader an appreciation of why critical thinking is such an important attitude not only for the evaluation of claims but in everyday life as well. Furthermore, this section is intended to provide some of the hallmarks of critical thinking for the evaluation of paranormal and pseudoscientific claims. Thus, such issues as double-blind procedures, the placebo effect, and the probabilities of strange coincidences (among others) will be presented. Also, this introduction to some of the hallmarks of critical thinking as it relates to the evaluation of claims will provide a reference point to compare with parts II and III of the book, where the question of why we all are vulnerable to uncritical acceptance of important information is addressed.

Also, please keep in mind that the list of topics to be covered in this introductory section is certainly not meant to be exhaustive. Thus, the reader should not finish part I and be under the false assumption that he now has all the required knowledge to apply critical thinking to any claim. Instead, think of the presented items as part of an all-you-can-eat buffet. Part I is simply the first plate taken back to the table, but there is much more left to be sampled. Perhaps the best thing about critical thinking is that there is always more to learn, just like there is always more to eat at the buffet! I hope, especially for the reader who is initially learning about critical thinking, that this section will whet your appetite for more and keep you wanting to refill your plate.

Chapter 1

CRITICAL THINKING IN EVERYDAY LIFE

What's Your Evidence?

Muddleheadedness has always been the sovereign force in human affairs—
a force far more potent than malevolence or nobility.

—Paul Gross and Norman Levitt,
Higher Superstition (1998, p. 1)

Let's take the following example to illustrate why critical thinking is important in everyday life. Imagine you have just taken a new job in a new city and want to purchase a house for your family to move into. You contact a real estate agent to show you available properties. The first house you view you absolutely love. The agent tells you the house is a "steal," is in a great school district, is in a very quiet neighborhood, and the market is "hot" so you should put in an offer today if you are interested in the property. At this point, what type of additional information and/or evidence does critical thinking demand prior to making an investment that can be hundreds of thousands of dollars and can have a major impact on your family's quality of life? Unfortunately, some individuals will simply make a decision without a critical evaluation of the evidence and put in an offer based upon nothing more than the emotional response elicited by the house (the house was "love at first sight") and/or reliance upon a potentially biased source (the agent typically works for the seller, not the buyer).

I would recommend, especially for such an expensive purchase, that a critical inquiry is warranted prior to putting in an offer. For example, is the house really a steal? It would be useful to see listings and recent sales of comparable houses to either support or refute the claim. For example, if the house is priced $50,000 above comparable houses, it is likely not a steal unless it is substantially upgraded (e.g., brand-new modern kitchen, more than one bathroom). Also, the potential buyers may want to see more than just a few houses to get a better idea of what the market is currently like and find out how long the houses in a particular neighborhood typically stay on the market. If houses are snatched up quickly after coming on the market, this is evidence of a sellers' market. In contrast, if most houses are not sold for long periods of time, it can indicate a buyers' market, which gives the buyer greater choice for a lower price. Also, you should find out how long the house you are interested in has been on the market. What if it has been listed for over a year—a clear warning sign that it is overpriced?

Likewise, could the agent have any bias in the presentation of the house? While most agents are honest individuals, they do work for the seller, which could lead to the positive information being emphasized and the negative qualities of the house minimized (i.e., a subtle bias in the presentation, as opposed to an objective analysis of the pros and cons). Inquiries about the quality of the school system are important from other objective sources or from other unbiased individuals. Also, the buyers may wish to drive by the property at different times of the day to determine how quiet the neighborhood is. What if the neighbors next door have loud dogs that are let out early in the morning and taken in only late at night? What if the neighbors on the other side play loud music into the night? Also, any formal offer should include a contingent house inspection by a home inspector that you hire (i.e., the person works for you). What if major cracks in the foundation are found that will cost tens of thousands of dollars to repair? I could continue, but I hope you get the idea at this point. Simply put, applying the evidence-demanding attitude puts the person in a better position to make an informed judgment, which helps to guide important decisions.

Of course, we do not always have time to apply critical thinking to every claim or decision in our lives, but for such a major decision as purchasing a house, the skeptical approach will increase the chances of making a sound decision. For those who rely upon faith or feelings in this instance (i.e., this house feels like home), they are playing a dangerous game. Thus, critical thinking has real-world applications and is not simply a way to test psychic claims or another term to be memorized from a textbook.

WHAT'S THE SPECIFIC EVIDENCE?

Perhaps the overarching hallmark of critical thinking is the evidence-demanding attitude, which then naturally leads to the specific methods that will be discussed. Simply put, critical thinking does not accept claims at face value but continues to dig for further evidence prior to evaluating the claim. To some degree, critical thinking is like the ideal detective, continually searching for further clues until the puzzle is solved or all the available evidence has been exhausted. One good way to start digging for evidence is to ask the following: What's the specific evidence to support your claim? Critical thinking does not stop there but should also rigorously evaluate the evidence once obtained. With that in mind, let's apply the evidence-seeking attitude to four separate claims.

1. First, is "repression" of traumatic memories common? This issue was of paramount importance in the late 1980s and early 1990s as the theory of "repressed memories" was popularized by such self-help books such as *The Courage to Heal* and given national attention through such vehicles as talk shows and made-for-television movies (which are shown on channels such as Lifetime). For example, the actress Roseanne Barr told a national audience on the *Oprah Winfrey Show* that "[w]hen someone asks you, 'Were you sexually abused as a

child?' there are only two answers: One of them is 'Yes,' and one of them is 'I don't know.' You can't say 'No'" (Loftus and Ketcham 1994, 176). Thanks, Oprah! Unfortunately, many people who were unhappy and/or suffering from psychological disorders started to believe that perhaps something traumatic happened in their past, and some sought out the help of therapists who specialized in "recovered" memory therapy.

Briefly, this theory said that in response to a traumatic event (e.g., a rape, childhood sexual abuse) a common response was for the mind to repress the event. Specifically, the individual would have no conscious memories of the event having ever occurred. Note that this is different than motivated forgetting, in which the individual chooses not to recall the event (e.g., a Vietnam veteran who intentionally chooses not to recall his war experiences), but certainly does not forget what happened. Of course, there are many reasons to question this claim at face value and to implement the evidence-seeking attitude. For example, Holocaust survivors did not repress their traumatic experiences (does anyone want to argue this was not a traumatic experience?). Likewise, children who have witnessed their parents' murder do not repress. The typical response of victims of rape and childhood sexual abuse is not repression. Those who witnessed people jumping to their death from the Twin Towers as they burned on 9/11 did not repress. Those who witnessed fifteen hundred people scream out to be saved and ultimately die the night the *Titanic* sank did not repress. Those high school students at Columbine who witnessed the murderers kill their classmates did not repress. (I could give many additional examples from the memory literature, but you get the point.) In fact, those who do witness or experience trauma have a much harder time forgetting, if anything. Thus, is repression a common occurrence? What is the actual evidence?

Unfortunately, prior to any critical evaluation of the evidence for the theory of repressed memories, individuals were being arrested and subsequently sent to jail based upon what is at best a speculative theory. Furthermore, in some states the law was actually changed (specifically, the statute of limitations was extended to begin on the date of the recovered memory). In fact, the numbers of individuals nationally that were being arrested and convicted spurred the creation of the False Memory Syndrome Foundation in 1992 (see http://www .fmsfonline.org/). Furthermore, "repression" was not limited to sexual abuse: therapists were "uncovering" memories of satanic ritual abuse (i.e., satanic cults performing human sacrifices, eating babies, and drinking their blood) and memories of UFO abductions, which typically included sexual experiments performed by aliens.

With that background information, psychologist Elizabeth Loftus and her colleagues set out to determine if false memories could be implanted in some individuals. This would be an important piece of evidence when evaluating the theory of repressed memories because an alternative explanation was that "repressed memories" were actually therapist-implanted memories. So, what is the exact evidence that memories can be implanted? Simply put, there is a plethora of studies by a wide range of authors who were able to create memories in individuals of events that never happened (see Loftus 2003). It's important to recognize that this body of evidence used very subtle suggestions to convince individuals of events that never happened in short periods of time. In contrast, therapists, typically over months and sometimes years, used extremely overt methods of suggestion to "recover" memories, such as hypnosis. Likewise, those who were recovering repressed memories of trauma did so using techniques (e.g., hypnosis, guided imagery) that have been subsequently demonstrated to help create false memories.

The first of these studies is commonly called the "lost in a shopping mall" experiment (Loftus and Pickrell 1995). In this study, the parents of the subjects were contacted and asked by the researchers to talk about three real events that occurred in the subject's childhood. The researchers then told the subjects about the three real events but added a pseudo-event (an event that did not occur). Subjects were told that their parents had also reported that they were lost in a shopping mall at the age of five or six for an extended period of time. Likewise, subjects were told that their parents had reported that they (the subjects) were very upset by the event, but that eventually an elderly person helped them reunite with family members. Interesting, approximately 25 percent of the subjects "remembered" the event (partially or wholly), and many of the subjects added additional details that were not given by the researchers. In this "lost in the mall" experiment, subjects have falsely remembered a wide variety of events that never occurred (see Loftus 2003 for a summary of these results from a wide range of researchers). For example, subjects have come to believe that they were viciously attacked by an animal, almost drowned and then rescued, caused an accident at a wedding, to name a few false memories. My personal favorite study was one in which researchers implanted a memory of the individual meeting Bugs Bunny at Disneyland (see Braun, Ellis, and Loftus 2002). This is referred to in the literature as the "remembering of an implausible event," as Bugs is a Warner Brothers character and would never be allowed at a Disney theme park. Readers are referred to Loftus's home page (http://www.seweb.uci.edu/faculty/loftus/) for many related articles.

So, what actually is the evidence for "repressed memories" being a common occurrence? If repression does occur, it is exceedingly rare (I am still unaware of a validated case) and is not a common response to trauma. Likewise, there is substantial evidence to indicate that false memories (i.e., memories of events that never took place) can be created in some individuals. Furthermore, the techniques used by therapists who "uncover" repressed memories are well known to create false memories. At this point, the theory of repressed memories appears best (and most parsimoniously) explained as memories being created, not uncovered. It was extremely unfortunate for everyone (both the individual and the family members) who uncritically got swept up in this idea that perhaps their problems were a result of a repressed traumatic event. Readers are referred to *The Myth of Repressed Memory* (Loftus and Ketcham 1994), *Making Monsters* (Ofshe and Watters 1994), and *Victims of Memory* (Pendergrast 1996) for further reading on this topic.

2. What is the specific evidence for the claim that a midlife crisis is a common occurrence? Specifically, a midlife crisis can be defined as a tumultuous struggle within the self about one's life and is often accom-

panied by radical changes in lifestyle (e.g., dumping the wife for a younger model, buying a convertible Corvette, wearing different, more trendy clothes). Many popular movies, such as *City Slickers* and *Father of the Bride,* have provided millions of people with so-called concrete examples of what happens to individuals, typically males, during middle adulthood. Simply put, many people believe that a midlife crisis is a common occurrence. I've wondered about the influence of the popularization of the midlife crisis. Specifically, how many people, because they believe it to be normal or expected, actually created a crisis for themselves? In essence, this can be a self-fulfilling prophecy.

However, this is a claim that should be subjected to a critical evaluation (i.e., what's the specific evidence?). First, researchers "have been puzzled by the resilience of the myth about the midlife crisis despite numerous studies showing no common pattern indicative of a crisis in the middle years" (Heckhausen 2001, 378). In fact, many individuals report middle adulthood as one of the best times of their lives for a variety of reasons (e.g., economic stability, more leisure time as their children are grown). Furthermore, research shows that personality is typically stable over the years. Thus, for those who do have a crisis in the middle years, they are also likely to have a crisis at other points in the lifespan, which indicates that there is nothing unique about the middle years in terms of a crisis. What seems to be the initial trigger for the myth itself are two books that popularized the notion of a common midlife crisis (Levinson et al. 1978; Sheehy 1976). Of course, the media helps to perpetuate the myth. However, empirical studies have failed to support what should be called the myth of the midlife crisis.

3. Is the time immediately after birth a special period for mothers to bond with their infants? For certain types of animals (e.g., sheep), a mother separated from her infant immediately after birth may show a wide range of deviant behavior (e.g., failing to care for the offspring). Interestingly, in the prestigious journal the *New England Journal of Medicine,* researchers investigated whether a similar phenomenon occurs with humans (see Klaus et al. 1972). This issue should be rigorously evaluated, as many mothers, for a variety of rea-

sons (e.g., Cesarean section, adopting a child), may not have the chance to bond with their infant immediately after birth. After the journal article was published, many popular books warned expecting mothers of the importance of bonding with their infants immediately after birth, in other words, they might show aberrant mothering behavior, they might not love their child as much as they would have if allowed to bond, and this lack of bonding could lead to long-term problems for the child.

However, critical thinking demands that not only do we ask where the evidence comes from (in this instance, a published paper in a prestigious journal), but we must rigorously evaluate the specific evidence. The evidence in this paper can be summarized as the following (I encourage the reader to review the paper personally): a confounded, small-sample ($n = 28$) study that used measures of material behavior that are not valid indicators of maternal bonding or attachment. Likewise, maternal behavior was only measured one time (about a month after the birth)—not exactly a time frame we can use to make lifelong predictions, and used a sample of mothers that was not reflective of the population at large at the time of the study.

I use this article when teaching research methods to allow students to pick out all of the methodological flaws (they are substantial, and undergraduate students with minimum training have no problem picking out the major flaws in the paper). To the authors' credit, they did recommend "caution." However, the authors also said that "these findings suggest a special attachment period in the human mother somewhat similar to that described in animals" (463), which helped to popularize this myth once the claim received media attention. Fortunately, subsequent research has helped to discredit the "bonding myth," but like so many myths, this one still survives today, despite the lack of any credible evidence to suggest that humans share this characteristic with sheep.

4. Are peptic ulcers typically caused by a bacterial infection? The consensus among the medical community in the 1970s and 1980s was that ulcers were generally caused by stress and/or excess acidity in the stomach. However, in the early 1980s, two Australian physicians,

Barry Marshall and Robin Warren, identified a new type of bacteria in the stomachs of patients with gastritis. This finding ultimately led to the hypothesis that peptic ulcers were caused by bacteria (see Marshall and Warren 1984). As pointed out by Thagard (1998), this idea was initially viewed as "preposterous," "absurd," and "outrageous." In essence, this was a theory that ran contrary to all scientific knowledge at the time.

This last example was chosen to provide the reader with an example of how the evidence-demanding attitude can result in obtaining evidence that supports even what is believed to be at the time a very speculative hypothesis. Note that the previous examples provided show how critical thinking can be used to discredit or find fault with specific claims (i.e., repressed memories, midlife crisis, bonding). Fortunately, in this instance, not everyone simply dismissed the claim but started to investigate the speculative hypothesis. Interestingly, the evidence started to accumulate, particularly double-blind studies (see chapter 3) showing that many ulcers can be cured with the use of antibiotics to eliminate the bacteria responsible for the ulcers, which supported the "preposterous" theory. In this brief example, what started out as what was commonly believed to be a ridiculous claim is now widely believed to be the correct hypothesis and is currently the widespread recommended and highly effective treatment for peptic ulcers. The important issue here is the process of critically evaluating claims, as sometimes what appears to be highly unlikely can ultimately be demonstrated as highly likely once the evidence comes forth. Thus, a critical investigation can be used to help both discredit or validate claims, as the goal of critical thinking is to ultimately ascertain or approximate the truth.

Chapter 2

EXPERTS

Benefits and Limitations

Many "men of science" stupidly assume that because they have been trained in the physical sciences or the medical arts, they are capable of flawless judgment in the investigation of alleged psychics. Nothing could be further from the truth. In fact, the more scientifically trained a person's mind, the more he or she is apt to be duped by an enterprising performer.
                                        —James Randi, *Flim-Flam* (1982, p. 7)

THE ROLE OF EXPERTS

The purpose of this chapter is threefold. First, to provide the reader with some basic information about experts. Second, to explain why seeking expert opinions is often an important element for the critical thinker who is investigating and/or evaluating a potential paranormal claim. Third, to point out the limitations of experts once they venture outside of their own particular field of expertise (see James Randi's quote above).

INTRODUCTION TO EXPERTS

First, it should be noted that many examples exist in which experts have been demonstrated to be wrong, and nonexperts have brought a fresh perspective to a problem, for example, the experts were wrong about the cause of most ulcers, and the nonexperts identified the causal bacteria. Likewise, we should always feel free to apply the methods of skepticism to an expert's opinion. Thus, experts, like everyone else, are not perfect and have limitations; in fact, the best experts tend to be aware of their personal limitations. Furthermore, an expert's opinion should ultimately have to stand on its own merits and not simply be accepted as truth because an expert "says so."

Despite that cautious introduction to experts, experts in general have some distinct advantages over nonexperts (see Glaser and Chi 1988). For example, experts (a) tend to perceive meaningful patterns in their field (e.g., reading an X-ray), (b) examine problems at a deeper level than a novice (e.g., cracks above windows in a house may be a sign of a moving foundation), (c) tend to look at problems from several different angles (e.g., what would be the best course of action for a patient with cancer), (d) typically process information quickly (if your brain surgeon has to open a book during the surgery, it is not a good sign), and (e) are able to self-monitor and self-correct if they are heading in the wrong direction. Also, people are not simply born experts; experts are made through deliberate practice that can take a number of years before expert performance in a particular field is attained (Ericsson and Charness 1994). Thus, experts have some particular skills and experiences that are valuable when making evaluations.

Remember, being an expert in a particular field does not make that individual immune from being wrong, but it typically increases the likelihood of the individual being correct. For example, if you take your car to an expert mechanic, the mechanic can misdiagnose the problem. However, the specificity of knowledge, combined with the years of experience that go into becoming an expert mechanic, give that individual a much better chance of diagnosing and fixing the problem with your car than a novice would have because of the qualities that accompany the expert mentioned previously. Simply put, being an expert gives that individual a distinct advantage compared to the nonexpert.

Furthermore, experts are familiar with the myths and misconceptions that accompany any discipline. For example, an expert in brain functioning is well aware of what is known as the 10 percent myth. The myth states that humans typically use only about 10 percent of their brains. Therefore, according to the myth, if we could only harness the remaining 90 percent, there is no telling what we could achieve. I have heard this myth repeated by psychics, motivational speakers, and in popular books and magazines. Of course, the 90 percent of "unused" brain is the areas of the cortex that are involved in such things as thinking, speaking, remembering, and learning. You can see the devastation to the "unused" areas in brain-damaged humans (e.g., strokes). Simply put, while there is redundancy in the brain that allows for reorganization, the notion that we use only 10 percent of our brains is a widespread myth but one well known by experts in brain functioning. Thus, experts have an advantage in spotting discipline-specific misconceptions.

Expertise can be more even specialized. Thus, even within a discipline, many experts may be unaware of misconceptions that more specialized experts take for granted. For example, in the discipline of psychology, I for many years repeated the myth that Eskimos (Inuit) have approximately one hundred different words for *snow*. Language is not my area of expertise within my discipline, and I (like many others) had heard this misinformation at some point and did not know that it is a myth (Burton 2001). In contrast, in other certain specialized areas, I am aware of misinformation that many of my colleagues accept as true (once again, expertise can be extremely specialized). For example, many social scientists believe that the data we collect for subsequent statistical analysis is almost always normally distributed— this is a myth (Riniolo and Porges 2000). My favorite article demonstrating that this is not so is titled "The Unicorn, The Normal Curve, and Other Improbable Creatures," which speaks for itself (Micceri 1989). Of course, we believe the myth has consequences, because there exists more precise statistical methods to analyze data when the researcher is more aware of the characteristics of the underlying population distribution than the statistical approaches that assume the data is from normally distributed populations (Wilcox 1998).

EXPERT HELP FOR CRITICAL EVALUATIONS OF PARANORMAL CLAIMS

It is important in a critical evaluation to seek out expert help when necessary and not to jump to a "psychic" explanation (or any type of far-reaching explanation) just because you do not have the expertise to explain what happened. (I personally cannot explain how the lights turn on in my house or how my car works, but I do not automatically turn to a psychic explanation.) Put another way, experts can help find more parsimonious (i.e., straightforward) explanations (see chapter 3) and are less likely to be fooled by repeated myths and misperceptions. Until simpler explanations have been ruled out, you are not allowed to move up to a more far-reaching explanation, as will be shown in the forthcoming examples. Expert advice for paranormal investigations is important because claims cross over such a wide range of disciplines and specialties.

For example, let's take one of the latest crazes among the New Age movement, fire walking. For those unfamiliar with fire walking, a wood fire is lit that ultimately results in a pit of extremely hot wood (approximately 1,000 degrees) once the flames subside. According to the New Age explanation, one must enter a higher or new state of consciousness (I'm not sure what that means) to keep one's feet from being burned when walking over the embers. There are training sessions that teach an individual to achieve this "higher" state of being before trying out fire walking. However, physicists (experts in this phenomenon) tell us that the reason people do not burn their feet is because the wood is a poor conductor of heat. As long as the individual walks at a brisk enough pace over a relatively short distance, her feet will not burn. As an analogy (I apologize, but I cannot remember the source of this example), you can quickly touch a cake immediately after you take it out of the oven and not burn your finger (i.e., the cake is a poor conductor). Of course, I do not recommend touching the metal pan (i.e., a great conductor). That being said, if the New Age crowd could do fire walking on a metal grill (as opposed to wood pit) without burning their feet, then I would say that is pretty impressive evidence to support their claim of entering a higher state of consciousness. However, you may want to alert the local emergency room prior to attempting this foolish act!

When specifically investigating psychic claims, conjurers (i.e., magicians) should be consulted, as many so-called psychics rely upon simple magic tricks. As James Randi (a former conjurer turned skeptic; see www.randi.org) has pointed out, many scientists over the years have been fooled by basic magic tricks because they did not possess the expertise in that area (no one is an expert in everything) and because some are too arrogant to think they can be fooled by an "average" person, which leaves them vulnerable to trickery (Randi 1982). Perhaps no other event illustrates this point better than what has now come to be known as Project Alpha (Randi 1985). Randi trained two young subjects in basic conjuring techniques and sent them to the McDonnell Laboratory for Psychical Research in St. Louis, posing as psychics. The hoax fooled the scientists—they believed the "psychics" were genuine—and helped to demonstrate how easily some scientists were deceived. Consulting an individual with conjuring expertise would have saved them from this embarrassment.

I personally think a good magician can fool a good scientist (one who has no training in conjuring) nine out of ten times if the magician is allowed to control the evaluation (perhaps this estimation is kind; 9.99999 out of 10 may be more accurate). Thus, a specific protocol that eliminates the possibility of cheating must be implemented when testing a "psychic" to eliminate the possibility of trickery. Perhaps the most interesting historical example of the importance of consulting a conjurer occurred during the early 1920s, when the prestigious magazine *Scientific American* was ready to award a $5,000 prize to a very skilled medium, Mina Crandon (aka "Margery"). Fortunately, Harry Houdini saved both *Scientific American* and several prominent scientists from making fools of themselves. More information about this investigation and the historic showdown between Houdini and Mina will be provided in chapter 8.

Moreover, it's important to keep in mind what spectacular illusions some of the best magicians (e.g., Lance Burton, David Copperfield, David Blane, Penn and Teller) can perform. I've seen Lance Burton make a women float, I've seen David Copperfield cut an assistant in half with a giant saw (no box either), I've seen David Blane reach inside a glass window, and so on. Simply put, there are some wonderful illusions that are performed by some extremely skilled magicians. What "psychics" do in comparison is essentially quite pitiful (wow, spoon bending!). I share Ian Rowland's (see www.ianrowland.com) opinion that many psychics are just frustrated, bad magicians. Thus, the individual skeptic, when venturing outside of his particular area of specialization, should keep in mind that experts can play an important role for the evaluation of specific claims.

THE LIMITATIONS OF EXPERTS

Finally, as previously mentioned, expertise and knowledge can be very specialized. Thus, those who are experts in one field or discipline may have no greater knowledge than the nonspecialist when venturing outside of their specific field of knowledge. For example, who would be better able to diagnosis physical illness, a medical doctor with twenty-five years of clinical experience who has stayed current in her discipline or a mechanic with no medical training or experience? I am going to personally rely upon the medical doctor. But then, who would you rather have work on your car, the medical doctor or the mechanic? Not surprisingly, I am going to go with the mechanic here.

What is important for this discussion of experts and expertise is that being an expert in one field (e.g., a medical doctor) does not necessarily make you an expert in another field. In fact, because knowledge is so specialized, experts (with very rare exceptions), tend to only excel in their specific fields of expertise. Thus, when experts go outside of their own fields (e.g., a chemist who gives financial advice), they typically have no greater insight than any other nonexpert, particularly when they have not even taken the time to familiarize themselves with the basics of the discipline. Put another way, expertise in one area does not necessarily translate into expertise in another area (remember, expertise takes hard work and much practice over a period of years).

Unfortunately, as Benda notes in *Trahison des clercs*, there is a "superstition of science held to be competent in all domains. . . . It remains to discover whether those who brandish this doctrine believe in it or whether they simply want to give the prestige of a scientific appearance to passions of their hearts, which they perfectly know are nothing but passions" (cited in Hayek 1944/1994, 210). Unfortunately, scientists have a long history of making excursions outside of their fields of expertise and giving opinions on topics in which they should not be considered experts and in some cases lack even basic competence. This is particularly troubling because (a) many people are likely to believe those with scientific training no matter what topic they are discussing, and (b) when scientists speak on issues in which they possess no expertise, the prestige of science still often accompanies their statements. So, we are more likely to believe the statements because of the source. However, this is a dangerous game, because once scientists move out of their own areas, they are no more likely to be correct than any other nonexpert (remember, many scientists have been fooled by basic magic tricks over the years), and the critical thinker should be aware of that distinction.

Finally, the training, methods, and experiences that an expert in a particular discipline receives may be beneficial for understanding and developing expertise in a new area. For example, many similarities exist between the collection and analysis of data within certain areas of psychology and economics (e.g., the importance of historical trends, sampling techniques, multiple interacting variables, responses to incentives and constraints), which provides some common ground.

Economists Friedrich Hayek (*The Sensory Order* 1952/1976), Thomas Sowell (*The Einstein Syndrome* 2001), and Julian Simon (*Good Mood* 1993), who are referenced in part III for their economic expertise, all made contributions to the field of psychology.

However, some disciplines (or specific areas within disciplines) have specific training and methods for evaluating claims that are not similar, which can exacerbate the problems when individuals venture outside of their specific field (once again, particularly when the individual has not taken the time to study the differences and the rationale behind the differences). For example, some biologists have generalized methods that are appropriate for biology (biologists are responsible for some of the greatest scientific contributions to our quality of life) but that are wholly inappropriate in other fields. Specifically, some biologists (certainly not all, as it is unfair to paint all biologists with the same brush) have for decades been making bold predictions of economic doom and disaster (see chapter 13), none of which have come true. (You should not be reading this material at this point, as you should have died long ago from starvation, environmental pollution, etc.) Readers are referred to the economist Julian Simon for many examples of experts in one field believing their expertise translates to another field (see *Hoodwinking the Nation* 1999).

Unfortunately, many irresponsible predictions, cloaked in the prestige of science, have been made over the years by individuals who are speaking on issues in which they often lack even a basic competence. One wonders if eventually legitimate concerns or problems that are a real threat to the general welfare will be much less likely to be taken seriously in the future. One can only cry wolf so many times before everyone tunes out. We, as critical thinkers, should never be afraid to evaluate the competence of the individual as it relates to the topic area in which they are presenting themselves as an expert (once again, I refer the reader to James Randi's quote at the beginning of this chapter).

Chapter 3

RESEARCH METHODS

*The Double-Blind Procedure, the Placebo Effect,
and the Law of Parsimony*

> *We do not expect such procedures from the amateurs, but we must demand
> them from the professionals. Otherwise, purported scientific discoveries
> become fanaticism, nothing more.*
> —James Randi, *Flim-Flam* (1982, p. 209)

DOUBLE-BLIND PROCEDURES

The scientific investigation of different claims can require different methods. There are specific tools to investigate "psychic" claims. Specifically, no valid test of psychic abilities can be given unless the test is given in a double-blind format, and any potential for any inadvertent sensory information given and any possibility of cheating has been eliminated. Simply put, the double-blind format is a procedure that ensures that both the participant (the psychic) and the experimenter are unaware of the correct answer. For a nice summary of the history of the double-blind procedure, see Bratman (2005). It should be noted that double-blind procedures are not recommended only for evaluating psychic claims but should be used whenever possible to evaluate a wide variety of claims.

There are three primary reasons why the double-blind format is so vital for an appropriate evaluation of psychic claims. First, this format ensures that the experimenter is not influenced by expectation. Thus, the double-blind procedure is also a method to protect experimenters from themselves, as there is a long history of experimenters seeing what they want to see (i.e., being influenced by expectations). For example, Rene Blondlot was a widely respected French physicist, who in 1903 "discovered" N-Rays shortly after a true scientific discovery of X-rays (a German discovery; there was a rivalry between various European nations at the time). N-Rays were believed to be a new invisible radiation. This radiation was observed by passing a fine thread coated with fluorescent material through a spectrum refracted by prisms and lenses. After Blondlot's initial discovery, other physicists detected N-Rays, which resulted in approximately one hundred published papers in the French scientific journal *Comptes Rendues* (Barber 1976). Subsequently, physicist Robert Wood of Johns Hopkins University was sent to investigate N-Rays by the prestigious journal *Nature*. While evaluating the legitimacy of N-Rays at Blondlot's laboratory (Hines 2002), Wood secretly implemented "blinded" procedures and demonstrated that N-Rays were not a true phenomenon (Wood 1904). In other words, N-Rays were an entirely subjective experience created by the influence of expectation (Randi 1982).

Unfortunately, the history of science contains many similar examples of blinded procedures not being implemented and the power of expectation creating erroneous results. For example, the widespread adoption of facilitated communication (FC) as a method to allow those with profound developmental disabilities (e.g., severe autism) to communicate provides a more recent case in point. For those unfamiliar with FC, it is a method in which a facilitator (a trained assistant) provides help to a nonverbal person to type letters on a keyboard by guiding his arm. The theory underlying FC is that many disabilities, which are believed to have severe cognitive impairment, were misdiagnosed. (FC has even been used with individuals with Down syndrome.) Actually, however, these individuals are trapped inside their bodies without a method to communicate (i.e., they are not cognitively impaired). Many viewed FC as a miracle method that would allow "misdiagnosed" individuals to finally communicate with the outside world. Certainly this is a theory worthy of an empirical investigation, as the implications are enormous if the theory is correct. Unfortunately, thousands of individuals were trained and practicing FC prior to any double-blind study to assess the validity of this method (i.e., is the individual's or the facilitator's expectation controlling the typing?). FC, when tested using blinded methods, has been empirically demonstrated to show that the facilitator's expectation controls the typing, not the individual with the developmental disability (Jacobson, Mulick, and Schwartz 1995; Wheeler, Jacobson, Paglieri, and Schwartz 1993).

My own research has looked into the possibility that, in psychophysiological research, those who edit data for artifacts are "blind." Without going into the nitty-gritty details, this is an interesting issue because data editing is typically necessary for many psychophysiological variables, editing contains some subjective decisions, and the editing itself for certain variables can substantially alter the final numbers. Thus, any editing should be blind to control for the insertion of bias that could literally make up results that look scientific but that could be nothing more than editing bias. In my study with Mark Yerger (see Riniolo and Yerger, in press), we investigated forty journal articles that used the psychophysiological variable respiratory sinus arrhythmia, a noninvasive marker of parasympathetic tone. Interestingly, only one out of forty studies in peer-reviewed journals used a blind editor. Thus, for the remaining thirty-nine articles, the possibility exists that results were influenced by an editor injecting a bias and creating results that do not exist. This study also illustrates the difficulty, even for researchers, in generalizing skills (all research psychologists are aware of the need for blinded procedures when subjective decisions are being made) to differing situations (other variables used blinded procedures in the articles where appropriate). In fact, in an e-mail follow-up to the authors of the studies— many of whom were highly accomplished researchers with numerous publications—the most common reason given for the lack of blinded procedures was that nobody told the researchers that blinded editing was necessary!

Simply put, when blinded procedures are not implemented, the possibility exists that results can be the consequence of expectation and not a true scientific discovery. In the N-Ray case, highly respected physicists recorded nonexistent visual sensations. Likewise, FC had thousands of facilitators unknowingly controlling the typing. The above examples should alert investigators to one of the most basic rules of research methodology: *blinded procedures should be implemented whenever possible* to control for the influence of expectation. As Michael Shermer (2001) has pointed out, one of the major differences between science and pseudoscience is the use of blinded procedures. Once again, this rule also applies to the investigation of psychics.

Second, the double-blind format ensures that the information is not provided to the psychic through other means, such as nonverbal cues. As an example, in 1949, a paper was published in the prestigious journal *Science* on the controversial topic of hypnotic age regression (True 1949). Hypnosis is still an unsolved issue in psychology, as credible evidence exists for those who believe that hypnosis is nothing more than individuals responding to social influences and expectations (i.e., people are playing the role of being hypnotized). Likewise, credible evidence also exists that people in the hypnotic state may be in a unique state of consciousness (i.e., the divided consciousness theory). With that in mind, the author wanted to determine if young adults ages twenty to twenty-four while under hypnosis could be age-regressed back to when they were ten, seven, and four years old. While hypnotized, subjects were asked, "What day is this?" on both their birthday and Christmas. Simply guessing the correct day of the week should lead to a correct response rate of 14.3 percent (a one in seven chance). However, the correct percentages ranged from 62 percent (age four birthday) to 94 percent (Christmas at age ten). These results provided strong initial evidence that during hypnosis, subjects could be age-regressed and taken back in time to accurately recall specific events. However, once additional researchers tried to replicate the study, they found accuracy rates (i.e., what day of the week is this?) consistent with chance.

So, what explained the inconsistency? In the final version of the paper, an editor changed the wording because of space concerns (just an honest editorial decision, no conspiracy here). Unfortunately, in the initial study, subjects were asked if it was a Monday, a Tuesday, and so on, by an individual who knew the correct answer (i.e., only a single blind study), not "What day is this?" as the final paper read. Thus, the possibility existed that subjects were able to read vocal inflections or were given other subtle nonverbal cues by the experimenter. The replications (i.e., performed using a true double-blind format) failed to demonstrate that subjects can be age-regressed and accurately answer. Likewise, the initial author also failed to replicate the results when using a double-blind procedure.

Third, when the double-blind format is implemented properly, it eliminates the potential for cheating by the psychic. Simply put, when performing an experiment with a psychic, it is wise to assume that the psychic will attempt to cheat. For example, let's say a psychic is going to try to determine what cards are in five sealed envelopes. For the experiment, we will use the famous "ESP cards" (sometimes also called Zener cards after their inventor). ESP cards come in packs of twenty-five (many magic shops sell them) and have five each of the following symbols: circle, plus sign, three wavy lines, square, and a five-pointed star. The cards are perhaps most famous today for their use in the 1984 movie *Ghostbusters* by the fictional character Dr. Venkman played by Bill Murray. The scene in the early portion of the film, in which Dr. Venkman is testing two individuals using the ESP cards, provides a wonderful example of why double-blind procedures are so critical in research.

The method I typically use is to take the cards into an isolated room at a random time and random location, assuming that the person being tested will try to cheat to obtain information. The cards are thoroughly shuffled while my hands are under a blanket where I cannot see the cards. The deck is cut, and a card is selected and put facedown into tin foil and wrapped up. At no time is there the possibility of anyone seeing the card, including myself. The card is subsequently sealed in an opaque envelope and then put into an additional envelope. This process is repeated an additional four times, and the remaining twenty cards are likewise sealed using the same procedure. At this point, I do not know which five cards are in the envelopes (i.e., the experimenter is blind). Furthermore, no one on the face of the earth knows which cards are in the envelopes (i.e., any potential subject is blind). Likewise, at no point are the envelopes in a position where potential cheating (i.e., the psychic could obtain information about them) could occur prior to the test for psychic powers. As an additional precaution, the envelopes are sealed in such a way that any potential tampering would be detected. However, if a psychic could consistently over many repeated replications identify the cards correctly at a rate higher than chance—in this instance 20 percent—this would provide strong evidence of legitimate psychic powers. I have never had anyone pass this simple test. Furthermore, as previously mentioned, the James Randi Educational Foundation (see www.randi .org) offers a one million dollar reward for anyone that can pass any type of double-blind test. Interestingly, at the end of the application, Randi is kind enough to give potential applicants one last important warning:

> Please be advised that several applicants have suffered great personal embarrassment after failing these tests. I strongly advise you to conduct proper double-blind tests of any ability you believe you can demonstrate, before attempting to undergo a testing for this prize. This has saved many applicants much time and work, by showing that the powers were quite imaginary on the part of the would-be claimant. Please do this, and do not choose to ignore the need for such a precaution. This advice is offered only so that the applicant might be spared these problems.

Randi has tested hundreds of individuals over the years. No one has passed. Ironically, many of the leading psychics refuse to be tested. Perhaps double-blind procedures give off negative psychic energy (see Riniolo and Schmidt 1999a for an empirical test of this hypothesis), but perhaps not!

THE PLACEBO EFFECT

There are few more robust findings in both the medical and psychological literature than the placebo effect. Simply put, the power of suggestion (the expectation that something positive will happen) can produce positive results. In the simplest example, imagine that you have a headache and ask a friend for some Tylenol. The friend goes to the medicine cabinet and returns with two pills that you believe will help relieve your pain; in fact, you were actually given an inert substance, such as sugar pills. Your headache goes away, not because of a drug with an active agent, but because of a belief that you were being given an effective treatment. Many studies demonstrate that the placebo effect is effective in treating anxiety, depression, and pain, to name a few conditions. Furthermore, there is also a "nocebo effect": the expectation that something negative will happen. Thus, imagine if you happened to tell your friend that the inert substance would not only relieve her pain but might result in diarrhea (the reader can figure out the rest from here). The nocebo can also be very powerful especially when the person has a strong expectation, such as really believing in the power of a voodoo doll to inflict harm.

Interestingly, using functional MRI (Wager et al. 2004), researchers have demonstrated that in brain regions that are sensitive to pain (thalamus, insula, anterior cingulated cortex), the placebo effect decreased neural activity. Furthermore, the reduction in neural activity was related to the decrease in reported pain, suggesting that the placebo effect is not simply a case of subjects complying with suggestion, but that placebos (i.e., the power of expectation) have the ability to influence brain functioning.

The placebo effect is important for the critical thinker because when evaluating the effectiveness of a claim (e.g., a psychic treatment for pain), the results need to be compared against a placebo effect. This is typically done with a rigorous double-blind study in which participants are randomly assigned to both a control group, which receives a placebo, and an experimental group, which receives treatment. If the control group and the experimental group both show improvement at the same level, the simplest explanation (see the law of parsimony following) is that the results are due to the placebo effect. Thus, to demonstrate the effectiveness of a treatment, the researchers must demonstrate meaningful improvement beyond a placebo effect. For example, Goldstein et al. (1998) compared the effectiveness of Viagra versus a placebo in a double-blind study for impotent men. For the placebo group, 22 percent of attempts at intercourse were successful (a nice placebo effect). However, at peak doses, the Viagra group had successful intercourse 69 percent of the time, well above the placebo rate.

In contrast, there currently exists a dramatic increase in the use of alternative medicine. Unfortunately, many types of treatment are promoted and implemented without any demonstration that the effectiveness of the treatment is greater than a placebo effect. In a randomized, double-blind, placebo-controlled study to test the effectiveness of permanent magnets to treat chronic low back pain, both the real magnets and the placebo magnets produced similar reductions in pain (Collacott, Zimmerman, White, and Rindone 2000). Of course, the same claim can be made about the effectiveness of "talk therapy" in treating such psychological problems as depression (see Dineen 1998; Watters and Ofshe 1999, *Therapy's Delusions*, for further details on this issue that always upsets my counseling friends). To date, I am unaware of any double-blind study using a comparable placebo control that demonstrates that "talk" therapy with a trained therapist is any more beneficial than "talk" with an untrained individual who has experience interacting with people but is believed by patients to be a trained therapist. (Please note that I do not mean to imply that all types of therapies give no benefit beyond a placebo.)

As another example to illustrate the necessity of double-blind procedures and controlling the placebo effect, let's briefly discuss subliminal messages. Specifically, subliminal messages are sensory information that is below the ability of our sensory system to process. For example, a dog whistle is an example of a subliminal message. The claim that we can be influenced by such messages is one that should be empirically tested prior to accepting the claim. Currently, subliminal tapes are widely advertised and sold as tools to help individuals with such issues as weight loss, improvement of sexual functioning, quitting smoking, and so on. In a clever double-blind study (Greenwald, Spangenberg, Pratkanis, and Eskenazi 1991), researchers tested the effectiveness of subliminal self-help audiotapes to produce the desired effect of either increasing self-esteem or improving an individual's memory in subjects who desired the outcomes claimed by the tapes. In this specific study, the researchers randomly altered the labeling of the self-esteem and memory tapes so that some subjects who believed they were receiving subliminal messages to increase self-esteem were actually listening to the memory tape. Likewise, some subjects who believed they were receiving subliminal help for memory were listening to the self-esteem tapes. The remaining subjects listened to the tapes that were correctly labeled. This design allowed the researchers to compare the effectiveness of the memory tapes and the self-esteem tapes with a comparison placebo group who only believed they were receiving the appropriate subliminal messages. After a month of use, results of the study showed an improvement in memory and self-esteem for all subjects who believed they were listening to the appropriate tapes. If the subliminal tapes really worked beyond a placebo, a greater improvement should have occurred for those subjects that listened to the real tapes as opposed to the mislabeled tapes. This did not occur.

THE LAW OF PARSIMONY

Another guiding principle for critical thinking when evaluating claims is the law of parsimony. The law of parsimony states "that among equally plausible explanations, the simplest is to be preferred" (Fernald 1984, 72). Thus, jumping to an extraordinary explanation, such as a psychic having genuine powers, should be avoided when simpler explanations have not yet been ruled out. However, when the simpler explanation is eliminated (e.g., a psychic passed a true double-blind test), this then allows for a more far-reaching explanation to be considered. For example, let's answer the following question. Why did the mouse eat the cheese? Until you have ruled out that the mouse was hungry (a simple explanation), the law of parsimony does not allow for a more complicated explanation to be given as much weight (the mouse ate because of self-esteem issues). However, if the mouse eats when full, more complicated explanations can be considered. It should be noted that the parsimonious explanation is not always correct, but the process is to proceed from the simplest first, then move up to a more complicated theory. Sort of like starting at the bottom of a ladder and working your way up the rungs.

Perhaps no other event in the history of science can better illustrate why it is necessary to use the law of parsimony than the case of Clever Hans the Clever Horse, who was known by virtually every literate person in the Western world in the early 1900s. First, some brief background information. The work of Charles Darwin had gained considerable acceptance in Germany and the United States by the late 1800s, and many people at the time in Germany and other countries became interested in the similarities between animals and humans. Furthermore, the general public, as well as scientists, became interested in the topic of animal intelligence. Darwin himself, in *The Descent of Man* (1874/1998), wrote, "There is no fundamental difference between man and the higher mammals in their mental faculties" (67). Many people wrote to popular magazines with stories of great animal intelligence that they had witnessed in horses and pigs, pet dogs and cats, to name a few. Even some well-respected scientists, such as the father of psychology, Wilhelm Wundt, got caught up in this trend of attributing humanlike intelligence to animals.

Likewise, George Romanes, Darwin's handpicked successor to apply evolutionary theory to the mind, published *Animal Intelligence* (1883), in which he tried to demonstrate the continuity in mental development between animal intelligence and human intelligence. His findings were based upon anecdotal observations using a technique called introspection by analogy—you assume the same mental processes occur in the animal's mind that occur in the observer's mind. This method is problematic and led Romanes to believe that fish and ants possessed complex human emotions such as jealousy, curiosity, and parental feelings.

With that information in mind, a former math teacher, Mr. von Osten, in Berlin, decided that he would begin to train his horse, Hans, in such things as spelling, reading, and basic mathematics. As Fernald (1984) notes in *The Hans Legacy*, Hans's master reasoned that if humans and animals share a common ancestor, "they must have comparable intelligence" (10). While this seems a ridiculous viewpoint today, it was viewed by many as reasonable at the time. Simply put, Mr. von Osten set out to demonstrate the similarities in intelligence between humans and animals. He firmly believed that his horse simply lacked the appropriate instruction (i.e., had been deprived of the opportunity to learn). If lessons were provided, Hans should be able to perform intellectual tasks similar to a human, as horses and humans share a common evolutionary heritage.

After thousands of hours of often painstaking and frustrating training and instruction, the horse, Clever Hans, eventually appeared to have learned how to both read and spell in German, perform mathematics, distinguish colors, tell time, and understand geography. Clever Hans eventually performed, free of charge, in front of large crowds by tapping his foot to indicate when he settled on his final response. Interestingly, his most impressive displays occurred when the human questioner was wrong, and Hans had to correct the often embarrassed individual in front of the rest of the viewers. Several prominent individuals tested Hans with equally spectacular results, as the horse was able to answer a variety of questions accurately. News of Clever Hans the Clever Horse quickly spread, and he received international attention in books, magazines, and newspaper articles. In fact, there was even a song written about him!

Prior to any formal investigation of Clever Hans, at least four major theories began to emerge to explain his abilities (see Fernald 1984 for further details). First, the newly discovered N-Rays were responsible for the abilities (see discussion of N-Rays at the beginning of this chapter). Second, if proper training is given, some animals have the potential to develop highly sophisticated mental abilities, perhaps even equivalent to humans. Third, Clever Hans was using mental telepathy (i.e., he was reading the minds of those in the audience) to successfully answer questions. Finally, the simplest explanation was that Mr. von Osten was using trickery, such as signaling the horse. Interestingly, many individuals "jumped" over the most parsimonious explanation and gravitated to the more unlikely ones (e.g., animals with training can think like humans).

However, most people skeptical of Clever Hans believed that deception was being used. Mr. von Osten vehemently denied this charge and was eager to clear his name. The Hans Commission, led by Professor Carl Stumpf from the University of Berlin and including thirteen distinguished professionals with appropriate expertise from a variety of fields, set out to settle once and for all whether or not Clever Hans was simply a fraud. The results from the inquiry clearly demonstrated that Hans could answer questions even without Mr. von Osten present. At the conclusion of the evaluation, it was unanimously agreed that no fraud was involved, which made international news. The following was published on page 2 of the *New York Times* on September 14, 1904:

HANS AN EQUINE WONDER.

German Scientific Commission Examines the Educated Horse.

A scientific commission which has been making a careful study of Hans, the educated horse, reports that the evidences he gave of comprehending handwriting, his musical and color discrimination, and mathematical work were performed under circumstances excluding the possibility of a trick.

Herr Bush, a member of the commission and a well-known authority on the training of horses, says the results obtained in the tests would be impossible by the usual drill methods.

The methods of the horse's owner, Herr von Osten, are pronounced to be those of a pedagogue rather than of an animal trainer.

While fraud was ruled out, Professor Stumpf believed that further inquiry was necessary. He believed there existed a more parsimonious explanation that could account for Clever Hans's abilities than the other more intricate theories being offered. For this job, he selected a graduate student working in his laboratory at the time, Oskar Pfungst. To test Clever Hans, Pfungst designed an experimental study with two conditions. First, a questioner knowing the correct answer would ask Hans a question (i.e., a "with knowledge" condition). In that condition, Hans could correctly answer questions, which was consistent with his previous abilities. Second, a questioner not knowing the correct answer would ask Hans a question (i.e., a "without knowledge" condition). In that condition (a double-blind condition), Hans failed miserably, as the horse did not even know its own name. According to Pfungst (cited in Fernald 1984, 66), "Hans can neither read, count, nor make calculations. He knows nothing of coins or cards, calendars or products, nor can he respond by tapping or otherwise, to a number spoken to him but a moment before." Thus, the hypothesis that Clever Hans had intelligence comparable to a human was quickly eliminated. Likewise, the "mind reading" and N-Ray hypotheses were also ruled out using simple experimental procedures.

So, if all of the previous hypotheses had been essentially ruled out by the experiments, what could account for Hans's incredible abilities to correctly answer questions? Further investigation using a series of well-controlled experiments allowed Pfungst to answer the riddle. Specifically, Hans developed the ability to read body language after the long hours of training. For example, most individuals leaned slightly forward when asking the horse a question (a cue to start tapping his foot), but leaned slightly backward when Hans came to the answer (a cue to stop tapping). Also, audience members leaned slightly backward when Hans came to the correct answer, which explains how Hans could in some instances correct a questioner. When performing for individuals or in front of a crowd, Hans was able to pick up on these very subtle cues, as horses have excellent vision. Thus, the parsimonious explanation was that the thousands of hours of schooling did not teach Hans how to do humanlike schoolwork but did reinforce and shape his ability to read extremely subtle nonverbal cues. Thus, Hans was not "clever" but was an extremely keen observer of nonverbal cues (he likely would have been a wonderful poker player).

Clever Hans, however, does provide us with several important lessons that should not be forgotten. First, the importance of implementing a double-blind procedure is evident. Even a horse could pick up subtle nonverbal cues that give information about a correct answer. Also, Hans demonstrates the importance of an empirical investigation. Note that many individuals were happy to accept Hans as being as smart as a human with very little investigative support. Finally, Hans demonstrates the importance of not automatically jumping to a complicated answer (e.g., telepathy, horses can think like humans) prior to excluding more parsimonious explanations. Note that if some had their way, horses would have been starting school along with children. Imagine that!

Chapter 4

WHY STRANGE COINCIDENCES ARE NORMAL, AND WHY THE CRITICAL THINKER IS WARY OF SECONDHAND SOURCES

> *Though it is unlikely that any* particular *sequence of events specified beforehand will occur, there is a high probability that some remarkable sequence of events will be observed subsequently.*
> —John Allen Paulos, *A Mathematician Reads the Newspaper*
> (1996, p. 50)

> *Sometimes I'm embarrassed by the work we do. We're supposed to double-check and get it right. We often don't.*
> —John Stossel, *Give Me a Break* (2004, p. 97)

THE PROBABILITIES OF STRANGE COINCIDENCES

Imagine that the odds of winning a "mega-jackpot" in Las Vegas playing the slot machines are one in fifteen million. Note that winning the jackpot with a single pull of the lever (or touch of a button) is an extremely unlikely event. However, in Las Vegas, thousands of people play thousands of slot machines over many days and sometimes weeks before the jackpot is won (i.e., millions of events occur). In order to place the eventual winner in the proper context, one needs to compare the total number of events (total times all slot machines were played) that occurred with the odds of winning. Note that it is not a strange coincidence that after fifteen million events a winner occurred. (Of course, sometimes a winner will occur with fewer events and sometimes with more events.) The important issue is that in order to evaluate odds in determining if the event is normal, it needs to be evaluated in the full context of number of events. The same could be said about the likelihood of someone winning the lottery (i.e., how many tickets were sold in comparison to the odds of an individual winning).

However, there are other events in which the actual probability of the event occurring is unknown (i.e., the problem of unknown probabilities). For example, imagine the following. Last night, you had a dream about an old high school friend that you have not seen or heard from in the last twenty years. Later in the week, while in the supermarket, you run into the old friend, or receive an e-mail out of the blue from this person. Many individuals interpret this type of strange coincidence as an event so unlikely that the dream must have indicated the ability to foresee a future event (i.e., a paranormal event). Before rushing to the paranormal interpretation, the likelihood of that coincidence has to be placed in a larger framework of odds. This can be difficult, because it is unknown how often events like this occur (readers are referred to Martin Gardner's work on this topic; see Gardner 1998).

So, how can this unlikely coincidence be explained as a normal event? First, keep in mind that the dream and the subsequent meeting of the friend are simply one of many potential coincidences that can occur in anyone's life. This is particularly true for those with active minds who are continually thinking about people, places, and events. For example, imagine that you think about an old high school friend but do not meet him later that week. That potential coincidence is an event that would be classified as a "miss," like pulling the slot machine to try to win the mega-jackpot but failing to win the prize. Interestingly, there are likely hundreds and thousands of potential coincidences that occur every day (and will occur in the future), which over the course of a lifetime can add up to millions or even billions of events. The majority of them "miss" and are quickly forgotten, as misses do not provide unique information (i.e., why remember a miss?). Because of the large number of potential coincidences that can occur, you are likely to get a "hit" for a very unlikely coincidence sometime in your life. However, since the misses are forgotten, a "hit" may feel like winning the mega-jackpot with a single pull of the slot machine, even though it is actually nothing more than an expected occurrence within the normal laws of probability. As a quick side note, when lecturing about strange events, the one consistent finding I have noticed is that if you ask the audience if they personally experienced such a strange occurrence, they would classify it as a billion-to-one shot; the older the audience, the greater number of hands are raised. I have interpreted this to mean that older individuals have many more potential chances for strange coincidences to occur.

As an example, imagine you blindfold an individual in the end zone of a football field and give her a bow and arrow to shoot. You then place a target the size of a dinner plate randomly on the 100-yard field. The chances of the individual hitting a bull's-eye with a single arrow are amazingly slim (i.e., an incredible coincidence). However, imagine that each person on earth was given a chance to blindly shoot the arrow. Once again, the odds of any single arrow finding the randomly placed target are miniscule. However, in the context of billions of arrows being shot, there is nothing unusual about one or several of the arrows hitting the bull's-eye. Of course, for those individuals whose shots connect (i.e., an incredible coincidence), convincing them that this is simply a normal event is harder than you can imagine. Perhaps David Myers (2002) has summed up this issue best by saying, "An event that happens but one in a billion people a day happens 2000 times a year. A day when nothing weird happened would actually be the weirdest day of all" (28). Simply put, incredible coincidences occur all of the time!

In addition, from a mathematical standpoint, coincidences (i.e., odd occurrences) are normal because random events will often "cluster" or "clump," which can give the appearance of something strange or supernatural but are simply expected in the larger context of probabilities. For example, take a piece of graphing paper and start to flip coins (i.e., a random occurrence). When the coin lands on heads, color the square black. When the coin is tails, color the square yellow. More often than not, you will find what appears to be non-random clumping of squares, but this is normal, because if you repeat the process (this can take a while) you will typically find more clumping. Likewise, take a jar filled with five hundred pennies and five hundred dimes randomly mixed together and empty the coins onto the floor from a distance of about five feet from the floor. Once again, normal clumping (i.e., a bunch of pennies together) is likely to occur again and again. (Perhaps the most effective way to demonstrate this is with the use of a random number generator, as the process can be repeated again and again, demonstrating how normal clumping actually is.) As Martin Gardner (1998, 15) correctly notes: "Normal clumping can be extremely misleading in statistical research. A town, for example, suddenly shows a high incidence of cancer. Is there something at work in the local area to cause this, or is it just random clustering? Astronomers find a large patch of space where there are no stars, or a long chain of galaxies. Are natural laws at work, or is it just clumping? It is sometimes difficult to tell."

My research (Riniolo and Schmidt 2000) also illustrates that statistical clumping or weird events are normal given enough opportunities. This article may be of some interest to psychology students, as it points out some of the pitfalls associated with using statistics packages to run large numbers of statistical tests and the inherent problems associated with interpreting results based upon a single small-sample study. Specifically, we collected data from thirty subjects on sixteen chance-related variables (e.g., flipping coins, rolling dice, drawing cards) and correlated all of the variables. This resulted in 120 individual statistical tests for correlations between the variables with a true zero relation (e.g., correlating the total number of heads from flipping a penny ten times with the total additive score from rolling five die simultaneously). Setting our alpha level at .05 to indicate statistical significance, we found in our initial study seven statistically significant relations (i.e., clumping of chance variables). After the initial study, we repeated the study an additional four times. Of course, none of the initial results were replicated, but we always found variables that, based upon a single test, were statistically significant. This is not surprising, since one expects chance-driven results, given enough potential events. Rephrased, odd occurrences are just normal events, given enough chances.

As a final example to show why placing isolated events is so important, let's examine a scam presented by Martin Gardner (1998, 11):

> Suppose you get a phone call from a stranger who says he knows the winning horse in a forthcoming race. It turns out that the horse wins. Later you get a second call from the same man, giving the winner in another race. He is right again. The third time he calls, he offers to sell you the name of the next winner. Should you buy it? Not if you know what actually has been going on. For the first race, in which seven horses ran, the man called seventy people, taking their names at random from a phone book. The first ten were given the name of horse *A*; the second ten, the name of horse *B*; and so on. Of course ten people will have been told the winner. Ten horses were in the second race. The man then called the ten who got the correct name for the first race. He gives each the name of a different horse. Of course one person got the winning name. Now he calls this person a third time with an offer to sell.

Without knowledge of the total number of events, you cannot make an accurate assessment of the odds and you may even deduce that the person on the phone has some mystical powers to predict the future, but when placed in the larger context of odds, there is really nothing unusual at all.

BE WARY OF SECONDHAND SOURCES (PARTICULARLY MEDIA REPORTS) AND VERIFY REPORTS FROM MULTIPLE SOURCES

If there is one thing that virtually all critical thinkers can agree upon, it's that the media is typically biased toward pro-paranormal explanations. In fact, the number of examples that could be given here are countless, so I will simply concentrate on one that is particularly egregious (see John Stosell's *Give Me a Break* 2004 for a wider range of examples of questionable reporting). However, please do not infer that I am suggesting that the reader track down every press release or perform a skeptical inquiry into all media claims. None of us has the time and energy necessary to achieve that goal. However, it is important (a) to have awareness that what is being presented in the media may be misleading or just plain false, and (b) in those instances in which you wish to ascertain the truth about a media claim, it is important to actively seek additional information as opposed to just passively accept information.

On Friday, April 2, 1999, I received an e-mail from the *Skeptic* magazine hotline, which is part of a mass mailing that informs skeptics of events and news on a regular basis. As part of the e-mail, Michael Shermer informed the readers that the television show *Unsolved Mysteries* (CBS) was airing a segment the following week (April 9) on a "Russian Psychic Healer," Nicolai Levashov. Apparently, the original segment was going to focus on two cases. The first case focused on a little girl with a recurring brain tumor who'd had several surgeries, radiation and chemo treatments, and "treatment" by Levashov. When the show aired, the child was at that point cancer free (i.e., a successful outcome). Of course, there is no way to know what caused her to be cancer free (was it the psychic treatment, the medical treatments, or a spontaneous remission?), but the implication was the psychic treatment was at least partly responsible.

The second case involved actress Susan Strasberg, who had breast cancer and had abandoned her traditional treatment in favor of Levashov's psychic healing methods. Unfortunately, Strasberg died of breast cancer prior to the final show airing. One would have assumed that both segments would have been shown, but they were not. Only the favorable segment aired, which is typically the way the media presents cases related to the supernatural. Of course, this should make us all wonder, if the media can so easily present "paranormal" stories with a clear bias, what other types of stories are routinely presented in the same manner.

I went to the *Unsolved Mysteries* home page on April 11, 1999, to see if any mention of Strasberg appeared in the synopsis of Nicolai Levashov. No mention was made of her on the Web site either. It makes for a better television show (i.e., more people will watch) if the pro-paranormal position is boosted. In fact, this type of reporting is unfortunate but commonplace when it comes to television programs related to the paranormal. To be fair, there have been some wonderful skeptical programs over the years (e.g., ABC's *Junk Science* & *The Power of Belief* hosted by John Stossel, NBC's *The Secrets of the Psychics*), but on balance, the pro-paranormal position is prevalent.

Of course, television is not the only form of information transmitted through the media that should be treated skeptically. For example, I was made aware of a press release (see *Skeptic* 8, 2000, 19) that was picked up by Reuters on March 15, 2000. In the press release it was claimed that "false memories" were "often independently corroborated" and that "a substantial portion of these memories have been corroborated." Thus, this research claimed to cast doubt on the prevalent claim that recovered memories were planted by therapists. I wanted to find out more information, so I e-mailed both the primary author of the study (to refer me to the appropriate article) and the press officer for the *British Psychological Society* (who sent out the media release). I was also interested in the accuracy of the quotes in the press release and who was responsible for presenting the information that way. The author told me via e-mail that "we do our best as academics to inform the public, and those who write press releases, but by their very nature press releases are notoriously short on detail however much we try to influence this." I subsequently called the press officer, who had a different version, implying that the press release was consistent with what the author wanted. Whose version was correct, I do not know. In any case, after a brief investigation of this issue, I wrote the following, which appeared in the "Skeptics' Forum" in the next issue of *Skeptic* (Riniolo 2000, 25).

SKEPTICAL OF SECOND HAND SOURCES

In *SKEPTIC* (Vol. 8, No. 1, 19) a claim was made that a substantial portion of recovered memories have been "corroborated." I e-mailed Dr. Andrews for the references for this extraordinary claim. In Andrews et al. (2000)—the article the press release was about—the authors state, "This study was unable to confirm or disconfirm the authenticity of the recovered memories. . . ." However, Andrews et al. (1999) attempts to find data that support the validity of recovered memories, but the evidence was based solely upon "therapists' observations of clients' reports." Thus, corroboration apparently is defined as unverified, second hand information. By this standard, the existence of Santa Claus has also been "corroborated." Interestingly, unlike the press release, Dr. Andrews was appropriately cautious of the results in her empirical paper (1999) and pointed out the methodological limitations. Unfortunately, I believe those who read the press release would interpret corroboration to mean that factual first hand accounts verified the accuracy of recovered memories (like DNA evidence that corroborates a suspect was at one time at the crime scene). Simply put, this is not the case. As always, skeptics are urged to be skeptical of second hand sources, especially for important issues such as the validity of recovered memories.

I was not the only one skeptical of the press release on this issue. On the same page that my brief comment was published, Mark Pendergrast (see *Victims of Memory*, 1996) does a wonderful job of further pointing out the scientific flaws that severely restrict the ability to generalize results from the Andrews study. Pendergrast correctly describes "corroboration" as "fourth-hand hearsay."

It is always important whenever possible to verify reports from more than a single source and to obtain information as close to first-hand sources as possible, especially if the possibility exists that the source could be either biased or self-serving in some respect. For example, many examples exist in the history of psychoanalysis of distortions that do not match the historical record in order to present a more appealing picture than what actually occurred (e.g., Freud's use of cocaine and advocacy of the benefits of cocaine have been minimized or omitted both by Freud himself and by sympathetic biographers; see Isbister 1985; Masson 1985). Let's focus on a legendary case in the history of psychoanalysis, the case of Anna O. (who was later revealed by one of Freud's biographers to be Bertha Pappenheim), which is still given as "evidence" of the effectiveness of the talking cure and repeated in many psychology textbooks. Briefly, Sigmund Freud's mentor, Josef Breuer, treated an attractive young woman who was suffering from severe hysterical complaints (mental deterioration, paralysis, memory loss, and visual and speech problems) that began when she was caring for her dying father whom she loved dearly, and her symptoms continued after his death.

Breuer treated Anna by hypnotizing her, and she would recall experiences that seemed to be linked with various symptoms. As the story goes, Anna O. referred to the therapeutic sessions as a "chimney sweeping" or "the talking cure." According to the "legend" of the case of Anna O., Breuer's treatment method resulted in her becoming cured (the importance of the event for psychoanalysis is the influence on Freud's subsequent implementation of a talking cure). However, Ellenberger (1972) used historical records (a medical report by one of Anna's doctors who treated her after Breuer) to reveal a vastly different version than what has become compelling "evidence" of the effectiveness of the talking cure. Specifically, when Breuer stopped treating Anna O., she was not becoming better but progressively worse. In fact, she was ultimately institutionalized and would sit for hours under a picture of her father and would speak of going to pay respects at his burial place. Furthermore, "Breuer told Freud that she was deranged; he hoped she would die to end her suffering" (Schultz and Schultz, 2004, 405). Simply put, the historical record, as opposed to the often repeated legend, indicates that Anna was not cured by Breuer, to say the least. Interestingly, although it is unclear how this transpired, Anna O./Bertha Pappenheim would eventually recover over time and lead a very productive life. (The West German government even issued a postage stamp in her honor for her contributions to the field of social work.) Yet, the legend of the "cathartic treatment" still lives on within the psychoanalytic community. However, this case does provide a very important lesson: Whenever possible, seek out as close to firsthand documentation as possible and keep in mind the potential that some information may be potentially biased for a variety of reasons.

Finally, it is important to reemphasize that a critical inquiry can not only cast doubt or discredit but can validate claims as well. For example, one claim that I had previously heard, without a specific reference, was that the psychologist John B. Watson (an important person in the history of psychology, who was very influential in moving psychology toward behaviorism and who is perhaps most well known today for the "little Albert" study in which he classically conditioned fear responses in a nine-month-old infant; see Watson and Raynor 1920) was so popular with his students at Johns Hopkins University that they actually dedicated a yearbook to him. While this is a minor issue, I was always curious whether this actually occurred, or was it like the case of Anna O., a legend that started and has subsequently been falsely repeated?

Fortunately, this is a claim that can be discredited, or verified, by seeking out firsthand documentation. Specifically, the Johns Hopkins yearbook, called the *Hullabaloo*, would provide the answer. Luckily, my sister, who is a traveling physical therapist, happened to take a job at Johns Hopkins for several months. After work one day, she found the archives where the old yearbooks were housed during the years Watson was a faculty member at Johns Hopkins (Watson was not at Hopkins for very long because he was forced to resign when his infidelity with a graduate assistant, Rosalie Rayner, became public knowledge) and she brought me the evidence, a digital file scanned from the yearbook, to validate the claim. On the dedication page of the 1909 *Hullabaloo*, Watson's first year at Hopkins, the following appeared:

To
PROFESSOR JOHN B. WATSON
as a welcome to our University
and as a souvenir
of the first Senior Class taught
by him at Hopkins
this book is
respectfully dedicated by
The Board of Editors

Watson contributed a short essay to the yearbook titled "Animal Psychology." In this case, actively seeking evidence helped to validate, not discredit, a claim. Thus, the next time I lecture about Watson in the classroom and tell students about his popularity leading to a yearbook dedication, I will know that my information is accurate, as opposed to having relied upon an unverified secondhand source. Interestingly, it has also been stated that Watson was voted handsomest professor by the Hopkins students, but I will leave it up to the reader to obtain the firsthand evidence for that claim.

SUMMARY FOR PART I

Part I was intended to persuade the reader that critical thinking has advantages in everyday life and that the evaluation of claims is the preferred method to ascertain or approximate the truth. This section reviewed several important hallmarks of critical thinking (not an exhaustive list), that will be useful as a point of reference when addressing specific issues related to inconsistent critical thinking in part II and part III. In fact, the last hallmark of critical thinking (be wary of secondhand sources), is one I grossly violated in regard to my previous beliefs about the Scopes Monkey Trial. However, I will address that issue in more detail in chapter 9.

Part II

THE EVOLUTION OF INCONSISTENT CRITICAL THINKING

The purpose of part II is to introduce the reader to an evolutionary-based framework that hypothesizes why all of us, even those trained to think critically, are inconsistent with our critical thinking performance in some situations. In order to accomplish this goal, chapter 5 will address the trade-off that can occur via the process of natural selection. Simply put, our evolutionary heritage results in abilities that are an overall benefit for survival and reproduction, but in certain circumstances these abilities can have unwanted influences.

The specific theory that will be elaborated upon in chapters 6 and 7 hypothesizes that our pattern-seeking tendencies as humans are complemented by a cognitive system (i.e., they are interconnected) that is biased toward strengthening and maintaining our current beliefs, both true and false. While the advantage of these biases from an evolutionary perspective will be elaborated upon, the unwanted influence for us as critical thinkers is that the biases can interfere with our ability to apply critical thinking and objectively evaluate claims in some circumstances. The most pertinent biases that interfere with our individual ability to evaluate claims will be reviewed from the large literature within cognitive psychology.

In chapter 8, although not the focus of this book, I will discuss the role of emotions and how emotionally based beliefs can interfere with our ability to skeptically evaluate evidence. Sir Arthur Conan Doyle and the Piltdown Man hoax will be used to illustrate the influence of emotionally based beliefs on objectively analyzing evidence.

Finally, in chapter 9, two case examples will be used to illustrate inconsistent critical thinking. After using as an example my own personal embarrassing abandonment of critical thinking in regard to the Scopes Monkey Trial, a second example involves a person with a brilliant mind and a reputation as an outstanding skeptic. These examples are reflective of the cognitive biases that we all possess, especially when our highly cherished personal beliefs are challenged.

Chapter 5

THE PROS AND CONS OF OUR EVOLUTIONARY HERITAGE

Can we doubt (remembering that many more individuals are born than can possibly survive) that individuals having any advantage, however slight, over others, would have the best chance of surviving and of procreating their kind? On the other hand, we may feel sure that any variation in the least degree injurious would be rigidly destroyed. This preservation of favorable individual differences and variation, and the destruction of those which are injurious, I have called Natural Selection, or the Survival of the Fittest.

—Charles Darwin, *The Origin of Species* (1859/2003, p. 89)

In contrast with other species, humans are not the largest animals on the planet. We are not the fastest runners, we do not have the most stamina or strength, and we have a variety of limitations compared with other species. This is not unusual, as the process of natural selection has resulted in every species having individual characteristics that are beneficial for survival and reproduction. Specifically, those traits that are beneficial to us as a species (i.e., humans) are more likely to be passed down to successive generations.

It is important to be aware that while natural selection results in the establishment of useful abilities for a particular species, often there is a trade-off, in other words, there can be unwanted influences mixed in with the overall beneficial trait that increases the likelihood of survival and reproduction. Let's take for example the cheetah, an animal with an obvious beneficial ability. The process of natural selection has resulted in the cheetah developing and ultimately possessing great speed, which has the benefit of allowing the cheetah to run faster than its prey. This individual characteristic of great bursts of speed, however, comes at a price. Specifically, the trade-off for the cheetah in obtaining this great speed is reduced stamina and strength. (Compare a cheetah with a lion or leopard; of course, the lion and leopard do not possess blazing speed, which is a trade-off for them.) So, if the cheetah does not catch its prey with the initial burst of energy, it is unlikely to have a successful hunt, as it does not possess the stamina to continue the chase. Simply put, perfection does not happen via the process of natural selection; rather, species possess specific useful modifications that more often than not increase the probability of successful survival and reproduction in response to unforeseeable circumstances.

Let's take an example of the trade-off that has resulted from the evolution of the human visual system as a graphic illustration of both very favorable and in isolated circumstances unfavorable outcomes. Note that the human visual system is a wonder of the evolutionary process. In today's society, this system allows people to track and (in some instances) hit a baseball, drive a car, have a sense of depth, and identify landmarks, among a wide variety of other acts. In most circumstances, the visual system provides us with the appropriate needed information and performs just fine. From an evolutionary perspective, the visual system has aided in our survival and reproduction in a wide variety of ways (e.g., to chase and kill prey, to spot a potential predator from a distance, to help identify a potential mate).

However, it is important to consider not only the benefits of the human visual system but the limitations that have also evolved. The process of natural selection does not produce perfection but has resulted in modifications that increase the chances of survival and reproduction. Specifically, one of the trade-offs for the human visual system is that in some circumstances we are prone to visual illusions (i.e., we see what does not exist in the physical world). As a personal example, when living in Colorado in the San Luis Valley as a new assistant professor in my first academic job, my wife and I used to have to drive over a mountain range to travel to the nearest big city. Every now and again, when no traffic was around, I used to stop the car and place it in neutral with my foot on the brake. The game was, are we going uphill or downhill? As a social scientist, I was well aware that perceptual cues can sometimes be very misleading, and the backdrop provided a variety of perceptual cues. Sometimes we guessed correctly, but sometimes when we guessed downhill, the car would roll backward and vice versa. Simply put, in certain circumstances our visual system provides misleading information, which demonstrates the imperfections of the system. However, in everyday life, we are typically not even aware that we may be taking in and interpreting visual information that does not accurately reflect reality. Thus, we can be wholly unaware, in certain contexts, of how our evolutionary heritage can influence us. In this instance, something as simple as evaluating "up" or "down" is

Figure 5

sometimes sabotaged by the evolutionary heritage of our visual system, which in most instances serves us well.

To give the reader a concrete example of how the visual system is imperfect and can mislead us without our knowledge, let's take a look at my favorite visual illusion (fig. 5). Please keep in mind that in a normal setting, you would not be aware that you were seeing an illusion, which changes the experience, but this illusion is so powerful that revealing this fact will not spoil its effect. With that disclaimer, look at the squares that are labeled A and B in the figure. Believe it or not, both squares are the same color (i.e., both are the identical shade of gray). Not convinced? Please check Dr. Adelson's Web site (http://web.mit.edu/persci/people/adelson/index.html) for a full explanation of this and other outstanding illusions. (No matter how many times I look at squares A and B, they still do not look the same to me.) Of course, virtually every reader has the ability to distinguish between different shades of gray in the majority of situations. This illusion, however, provides a powerful example of how our evolutionary heritage can influence our ability to accurately evaluate evidence in this particular circumstance. In chapter 7, we will discuss how our cognitive system, because of the built-in biases that humans possess to support and maintain beliefs, can likewise hinder our ability to accurately evaluate evidence in certain situations.

For anyone interested in additional examples of how our visual system can mislead us, I would encourage you to look in any introductory psychology or cognitive psychology textbook and turn to the chapter on sensation and perception. I also highly recommend Al Seckel's *The Art of Optical Illusions* (2000), and there are many wonderful Web sites devoted to visual illusions (e.g., http://www.eyetricks.com/). Of course, many magic tricks, such as the one in which swords are thrust into a box with the assistant inside, take advantage of visual illusions by which the human visual system is prone to be misled. The box looks very small because of the perceptual cues, which is the illusion, but in reality it is large enough for the assistant to move back and forth to avoid the swords, which are put into the box in a set order.

As we move ahead to the next chapters, the important issue is that the process of evolution should be viewed as providing a species with useful qualities that increase the chances of survival and reproduction (in most instances, the visual system provides the necessary and relevant information), but that there is also a trade-off that can be accompanied by unwanted influences. The following chapters will argue that our ability to think critically is influenced by our evolutionary heritage and that sometimes we will be unaware that this is occurring, as when we are fooled by visual illusions.

Chapter 6

HUMANS

The Great Pattern Seekers

The tendency to impute order to ambiguous stimuli is simply built into the cognitive machinery we use to apprehend the world. It may have been bred into us through evolution because of its general adaptiveness: We can capitalize on ordered phenomena in ways that we cannot on those that are random. The predisposition to detect patterns and make connections is what leads to discovery and advance. The problem, however, is that the tendency is so strong and so automatic that we sometimes detect coherence even when it does not exist.
—Thomas Gilovich, *How We Know What Isn't So* (1993, p. 10)

As previously mentioned, evolution (via the process of natural selection) results in adaptations that are beneficial for survival and reproduction. For humans, one of those traits, which has been passed down through the process of natural selection, is that "[w]e evolved to be skilled, pattern-seeking, causal-finding creatures. Those who were best at finding patterns (standing upwind of game animals is bad for the hunt, cow manure is good for the crops) left behind the most offspring. We are their descendants" (Shermer 2001, xxiv). Of course, those who did not identify important patterns (e.g., that type of snake is poisonous) were much less likely to survive and reproduce.

This theory that humans are a pattern-seeking species has been enforced by a wide variety of authors within the skeptical community and by evolutionary psychologists who attempt to explain current human behavior within an evolutionary framework. I agree with this interpretation and believe that pattern seeking is one of the defining characteristics for us as humans (like the large neck is a defining characteristic of the giraffe).

Let's take the following real-world example of how our evolutionary heritage and the desire of humans to seek and establish patterns can influence us today. Imagine that you went on a first date last night. You had an absolutely wonderful time and want to see the person again for a second date. At the end of the evening, your date clearly said to you that he/she would call you tomorrow to set up plans for the weekend. What starts to happen the next day as the hours pass from the morning, to afternoon, to late in the evening if the person does not call? Typically, our evolutionary heritage (i.e., our pattern-seeking tendencies) starts to come out. Our minds can start to produce a wide variety of potential explanations as to why the person has not called in order to attempt to identify the correct pattern. Were they hit by a car and are now lying in a coma in the hospital? Did they not really have a good time and lied that they would call? The number of potential hypotheses that can occur is substantial, as our mind attempts to figure out the answer because we are a pattern-seeking species. Sometimes we identify the correct pattern, and sometimes we do not. However, the overall benefits from our pattern seeking were advantageous in the struggle for survival and reproduction, which is why it was passed on to successive generations and is still with us today.

Thus, from an evolutionary perspective, we are programmed to seek and establish relations among variables. However, just like the human visual system has both pros and some cons (see chapter 5), our pattern-seeking tendencies also have benefits and drawbacks (once again, the benefits outweigh the drawbacks). Unfortunately, in seeking and trying to establish patterns, we are likely to identify not only real relations (e.g., dark clouds are associated with rain and provide us with information that it would be beneficial to seek shelter) but meaningless or false patterns as well (e.g., a gambler "blowing" on dice prior to rolling them). Identifying a nonexistent or wrong pattern can be counterproductive for the individual (e.g., believing it is better to hunt upwind) or can simply not influence survival or reproduction in any meaningful way. Of course, some false patterns may in certain circumstances have some positive benefits (e.g., an athlete wearing "lucky socks" may result in the individual playing with more confidence during the game). Likewise, the consequences of not identifying a true pattern (e.g., not avoiding the poisonous snake) are typically more dangerous or of greater consequence than identifying a false pattern (e.g., avoiding a nonpoisonous snake), which helps to further explain why overall pattern seeking has been a net benefit from an evolutionary perspective.

Thus, the process of natural selection has resulted in humans being a pattern-seeking species that contributes to the development of beliefs, both true and false about how the world works. Although beyond the scope of discussion here, pattern-seeking abilities can contribute to the development of individual beliefs in several ways. For example, the individual personally identifies a pattern that leads to a belief (i.e., a direct route to creating a belief). Likewise, the development of our beliefs can also be influenced by patterns identified by others (allowing us to take advantage of others' pattern-seeking abilities), some of which are passed down from generation to generation (i.e., an indirect route to creating a belief). To keep this discussion manageable, let's assume that pattern seeking contributes to beliefs, both true and false, in several ways, both directly and indirectly, and that overall humans' pattern seeking resulted in knowledge that was a net gain for survival and reproduction (e.g., the useful information gained from pattern seeking outweighs the disadvantages from misidentifying patterns and creating false beliefs).

AN EXAMPLE OF PATTERN SEEKING GONE WRONG: THE GAMBLER'S FALLACY

At this point, I would like to provide the reader with an example of how our pattern-seeking heritage has the trade-off feature of helping to identify a false or wrong pattern in today's society. Once again, our pattern-seeking tendencies had a net gain, as humans are skilled at finding causal relations, but let's focus on how this tendency can mislead to reinforce the notion that natural selection does not result in perfection. The concept known as the "gambler's fallacy" helps to demonstrate how our pattern-seeking behavior can mislead us in certain circumstances. Simply put, humans often have inaccurate perceptions about random processes and try to identify patterns where none exist (the definition of a random pattern is the lack of any useful information). Let's look at the following example as an illustration of the gambler's fallacy:

> During your vacation in Las Vegas over the holiday season, you are observing a fair roulette table (i.e., the table has an equal chance of coming up "red" or "black"). You observe that the previous six spins have all come up "red." On the next spin, placing your money on which color would provide you the better opportunity to win?

One of the problems is that our evolutionary heritage has made us pattern seekers, even when no pattern with meaning exists. Thus, the above pattern we have observed is that a 50/50 event has gone one way six times in a row. The odds of this occurring by chance are one in sixty-four (i.e., $\frac{1}{2} \times \frac{1}{2} \times \frac{1}{2} \times \frac{1}{2} \times \frac{1}{2} \times \frac{1}{2}$). At this point, many gamblers will place their bets, often increasing the wager, on black. The erroneous belief (the gambler's fallacy) is that random processes are self-correcting. Simply put, black must be "due" to come up, because red has come up six times in a row. In fact, the plain truth is that the odds of the next spin coming up red or black is still 50/50, no matter what the previous pattern was. Of course, the roulette dealer is not interested in which color you bet on in a chance game, she is concerned only that you do bet. Over the long run, the odds of red/black coming up is 50 percent because there is no self-correcting mechanism! The casino makes money by paying out slightly less for a winning bet than it keeps for a losing bet, but this adds up to a substantial profit in the long run. Ever notice how many new hotels keep popping up in Las Vegas?

Not convinced? Interestingly, research demonstrates that misconceptions about random processes survive despite considerable contradictory evidence. Here is a simple exercise you can try at home (it can be time consuming). Simply start flipping coins and calculate the probability of heads coming up after three consecutive tails. If you repeat this process to the point that you have a large sample, you will find out that the probability of heads occurring is still 50 percent. Note that for the roulette table or the coins to have a self-correcting mechanism, this would imply that "a fair roulette table can remember if previous spins were black or red" and "that coins have a memory to balance out heads and tails" (Riniolo and Schmidt 1999, 199). Of course, for the gambler, the notion that they are "due" can be hard to resist. However, in true chance games (i.e., no card counting!), the probability of correctly guessing the next event does not increase based upon previous events. These misinterpretations are part of the trade-off that has resulted in our species developing pattern-seeking skills, which in the long run were beneficial for survival and reproduction but in today's society can mislead us when we try to attach meaning to random events.

FRANZ JOSEF GALL: THE PATTERN SEEKER

Franz Josef Gall (1758–1828) provides an interesting case example of how our pattern-seeking heritage resulted in the identification of both true and false patterns. Unfortunately for Gall, the history of science typically ignores the true patterns that he discovered and remembers him only for the false patterns. First, Gall was a remarkable anatomist, as he identified the fibers that cross from one side of the brain and connect with the opposite side of the spinal cord (contralaterality). This finding explains why a stroke on the left side of the brain can result in paralysis on the right side of the body, and vice versa. Please note that when Gall made this discovery in the 1800s, the instruments were very crude by today's standards. Furthermore, Gall was also a comparative anatomist and he investigated a wide variety of different species in addition to normal human adults, brain-damaged adults, and children. Gall properly identified the general pattern that larger brains are associated with greater mental abilities. This discovery was the evidence needed to convince the scientific community at the time that mental functioning was the result of brain activity. This seems like an obvious finding now, but many important scientific discoveries seem obvious with the benefit of hindsight (doesn't gravity seem obvious?). Simply put, some of Gall's achievements should have solidified his place in the history of science as one of the truly great individuals.

Furthermore, Gall also came to believe that the brain consisted of specialized parts that were associated with specific emotional, behavioral, and intellectual functions. He posited that those parts of the brain that were well developed and unusually large would be associated with greater abilities and more pronounced psychological qualities. (In general, Gall is the first to argue for cortical localization, another important finding.) Unfortunately, Gall also believed (inaccurately) that an individual's skull is a mirror image of the underlying brain. Thus, he believed that by searching for bumps on the skull, one could tell which areas of the brain were large, and so he set out to identify brain areas associated with specific abilities and psychological qualities.

The story at this point turns into a classic example of how our evolutionary heritage to identify patterns can mislead us when dealing with a random process. Gall searched for bumps and indentations on various individual skulls and subsequently mapped out what he believed was the corresponding brain regions and psychological qualities.

This "skull reading" is known as phrenology and was subsequently popularized by Johann Spurzheim (1776–1832) and George Combe (1788–1858). This pseudoscientific craze in the early to mid-1800s convinced thousands of practitioners who also saw a "real pattern" where none existed. Of course, the skull is made of bone, while the brain is like Jell-O. There is no way Jell-O can cause "bumps" to occur, no matter how large individual portions of the brain are. With Gall, we see a brilliant individual accurately identifying some patterns and also misidentifying the random information of bumps on the skull being associated with psychological qualities. Unfortunately, Gall is typically remembered in the history of science as nothing more than a joke: the fool who gave us phrenology. Interestingly, Gall's many other important contributions listed previously are typically not mentioned when his name comes up. Readers are referred to Fancher (1996) for further details regarding Gall and phrenology.

SUMMARY

Our evolutionary heritage has resulted in humans being a pattern-seeking species, which is an overall benefit, as it allows us to identify useful causal relations that increase the chances of survival and reproduction. Of course, while our pattern-seeking abilities lead to many true beliefs about how the world works (e.g., many birds migrate south for the winter), it also leads to some false beliefs (e.g., the gambler's fallacy). Thus, humans have a combination of true and false beliefs that have resulted from our pattern-seeking tendencies. A more important issue, which will be discussed more fully in the next chapter, is that pattern-seeking tendencies, if left unchecked, would simultaneously begin to undermine our beliefs. This would in turn reduce the advantage for survival and reproduction unless they were complemented by a cognitive system that is designed to take advantage of our ability to capitalize on the important information in ordered patterns. However, this requires a biased cognitive system designed to strengthen and maintain current beliefs. Unfortunately, interpreting information within a biased cognitive system also has a trade-off, especially for us as critical thinkers, which is inconsistent critical thinking.

Chapter 7

THE INTERCONNECTEDNESS OF OUR PATTERN-SEEKING HERITAGE WITH A BIASED COGNITIVE SYSTEM

We must, however, acknowledge, as it seems to me, that man with all his noble qualities, with sympathy which feels for the most debased, with benevolence which extends not only to other men but to the humblest living creature, with his god-like intellect which has penetrated into the movements and constitution of the solar system—with all these exalted powers—Man still bears in his bodily frame the indelible stamp of his lowly origin.
—Charles Darwin, *The Descent of Man* (1874/1998, p. 643)

Contemporary evolutionary theory within cognitive psychology hypothesizes that "cognitive errors result from *adaptive biases* that exist in the present because they led to survival and reproductive advantages for humans in the past" (Haselton and Buss 2000, 81). Thus, the cognitive biases that have evolved should produce predictable errors and still persist today. To use Darwin's terminology, part of the "indelible stamp" in humans is our cognitive biases. Likewise for the individual, we are not typically aware that our biases may be influencing us in a particular situation. These biases, while advantageous from an evolutionary perspective, have the unwanted influence for us today of sometimes interfering with our ability to accurately perceive and objectively evaluate evidence.

As an example of a cognitive error that was adaptive from an evolutionary standpoint but currently interferes with our ability to objectively evaluate evidence, let's look at the following case. Specifically, there exists evidence that males typically over-infer sexual interest from a potential female partner (Abbey 1982). Thus, males will often over-interpret such cues from females as simple friendliness, a smile, or a touch on the shoulder as evidence of sexual interest. However, within the framework of adaptive biases, the advantage for males possessing this cognitive bias is as follows: "Ancestral men who tended to falsely infer a prospective mate's sexual intent (a false-positive error) paid the fairly low costs of failed sexual pursuit: perhaps some lost time and wasted courtship effort. In contrast, men who tended to falsely infer that a woman lacked sexual intent (a false-negative error) paid the costs of losing a sexual opportunity and hence a reproductive opportunity" (Haselton and Buss 2000, 82–83). In contrast, females have developed their own adaptive bias related to inferring cues from a potential partner. Specifically, "ancestral women suffered greater costs when they erred by falsely inferring a prospective mate's commitment" (88). Today, the persisting cognitive bias is that women tend to underestimate men's commitment. Thus, evolution has biased the cognitive system of both males and females, depending upon their reproductive roles. The important issue for further discussion, however, is that cognitive biases are still with us today. In many contexts we are not only unaware of the biases that we possess but when the biases are influencing our ability to evaluate information (remember squares A and B from the illusion in chapter 5?). In essence, human biases influence our beliefs and can interfere with our ability to objectively evaluate information.

INTERCONNECTED: PATTERN SEEKING AND A BIASED COGNITIVE SYSTEM

The theory that pattern seeking provided an evolutionary advantage for humans should not be considered solely in isolation but needs a larger framework to more comprehensively explain the overall implications. The beliefs derived from pattern seeking provide an evolutionary advantage because they guide actions increasing the probability of survival and reproduction. An example is the belief that hunting downwind is beneficial because it increases the probability of successfully killing prey. Confidence in individual beliefs directly influences the likelihood that the beliefs are acted upon (e.g., the gambler who has great confidence he is "due" is more likely to wager). Thus, to maximize the evolutionary advantage of pattern-seeking skills by increasing the likelihood we would capitalize on the useful information identified, humans also developed or already possessed a cognitive system that *is biased toward strengthening and maintaining beliefs*. This book theorizes that pattern seeking and a biased cognitive system became interconnected at some point, which contributed to each persisting today.

In order to explain how pattern seeking and a biased cognitive system toward strengthening and maintaining beliefs are interconnected and beneficial together within an evolutionary framework to maximize the advantages of pattern-seeking tendencies, let's look at the following example. Imagine two individuals, one with a bias to maintain beliefs, another with a lesser or no bias, who have recently correctly identified a useful pattern and ultimately developed a belief that a specific time of day is the best time to get water from rivers and streams (i.e., this time of day results in the least likelihood of running into potential life-threatening predators). Thus, they each used their pattern-seeking heritage to establish a belief that at this point results in actions that increase the likelihood of survival.

However, in nature, no pattern is perfectly predictable, as exceptions to the rule occur at various times and some disconfirming evidence can always be found (e.g., sometimes when the dark clouds roll across the sky, it does not rain), but identifying the overall pattern and acting on that information is advantageous in the long run. Subsequently, a predator is identified during the believed "safe time" (i.e., an exception to the overall pattern). In this theoretical scenario, the individual with the stronger bias to maintain beliefs is more likely to continue the beneficial actions in the future (i.e., the next day she will go to the stream at the time of day with the least probability of encountering a predator) because the biased cognitive system is structured to maintain beliefs (i.e., confidence in the accuracy of the belief will remain high) and is resistant to inconsistent information once the belief is formed and established.

In contrast, the individual without the bias (or with a lesser bias) would be more likely to be influenced by the discrediting information and lose confidence or alter or abandon his belief, resulting in a lower probability of not continuing the beneficial action. Thus, he would be more likely to have a greater probability of meeting a predator in the future, which decreases the chances for survival. Simply put, since we are skilled pattern seekers who find important relations, a bias toward maintaining the beliefs that we have identified results in an overall benefit because it does not allow our beliefs to be easily influenced by minimal disconfirming evidence that always exists in nature (and often will be identified by us as a pattern-seeking species). While this does not mean that we cannot change our beliefs after they are formed (seeing a predator on many consecutive days during what was believed to be the "safe" time would likely result in a changing of that belief), it does imply that it can take substantial evidence to influence or ultimately change a belief.

Likewise, the amount of discrediting evidence it would ultimately take to modify or change a belief would depend upon the amount of evidence supporting the belief itself. Thus, those who possessed or had a greater bias toward strengthening current beliefs would have collected a greater body of evidence supporting and reinforcing the belief over time, making the belief more resistant to minimal disconfirming evidence. Once again, a stronger bias toward strengthening current beliefs would increase the chances of continuing the overall beneficial actions in the future. In the theoretical case presented above, this means increasing the chances of avoiding life-threatening predators.

Once we develop and reinforce a belief about how the world works, it would be counterproductive to continually challenge and change our beliefs in response to minimal disconfirming evidence (i.e., seeing the predator just one time). This would result in an indecisiveness that would limit our ability to act on information, because our confidence in our beliefs and the beliefs themselves would be under constant revision. Once again, there is no evolutionary advantage for a pattern-seeking species unless information is put into action (what good is believing that hunting downwind is advantageous unless that belief is accompanied by the behavioral actions?). In some situations, our pattern-seeking tendencies would simultaneously undermine the very same beliefs that we identified and would overall serve us well. Just as a universal skepticism (i.e., being skeptical of everything) eventually becomes counterproductive, so would pattern-seeking tendencies in a completely objective cognitive system. Without a biased cognitive system toward strengthening and maintaining beliefs, the advantages of our pattern-seeking abilities are reduced because we would be less likely to act on information. Thus, the biases toward strengthening and maintaining beliefs serve as a check to keep our pattern seeking from undermining our beliefs and ultimately reducing the probability that our beliefs will be acted upon.

Thus, *we are not only the decedents of the best of the pattern seekers but the decedents of those who were biased toward strengthening and maintaining beliefs.* This increases the likelihood that we will act on information. The two are interconnected. Of course, the unwanted influence or trade-off that natural selection has left humans with today is that both true beliefs and false beliefs will be more resistant to change as the biases cannot discriminate between accurate and inaccurate reflections of reality but instead support all beliefs (overall, this was a net gain). In certain situations, some beliefs will be rigorously defended, especially those for which we have large cognitive and emotional investments to support the beliefs. This framework helps to explain why even in the face of substantial discrediting evidence people can continue to believe in very strange things (e.g., the gambler's fallacy, the accuracy of psychic predictions). Specifically, for us as critical thinkers, evolution's unwanted influence is that we have a cognitive system that is biased and can in some instances influence our critical thinking performance. In essence, the predictable error for us as critical thinkers is inconsistent critical thinking for all of us.

So, does any evidence exist to demonstrate that once we have established a belief our cognitive systems are biased toward strengthening and maintaining our current beliefs, whether true or false? Simply put, yes! While the cognitive literature is flooded with research studies that point to a wide variety of biases that exist in the human cognitive system, the three most relevant types of bias that are interconnected with our pattern-seeking tendencies for the strengthening and maintenance of beliefs will be discussed here: the confirmation bias, biased assimilation, and belief perseverance. For readers interested in how other types of biases influence our everyday judgments, Thomas Gilovich's (1993) *How We Know What Isn't So* is highly recommended.

OUR BIASED COGNITIVE SYSTEM

Confirmation Bias

First, humans look for evidence that is already consistent with their beliefs, including both true and false beliefs. Likewise, people typically do not seek out information that will discredit the beliefs they currently hold. Psychologists call this a confirmation bias. A useful way of conceptualizing the confirmation bias is to think of the way a prosecuting attorney puts together a case in the American justice system once the belief has been established that the defendant is guilty. The prosecutor's job is to gather and present the evidence that is consistent with "guilt" (i.e., to seek evidence to support a position), not to seek out the evidence that contradicts that belief (that is the defense attorney's job). Of course, the confirmation bias is less conscious (i.e., people are typically unaware of the bias) than in the example just given. However, the concept is correct. We attempt to establish what we already believe (i.e., our pattern-seeking heritage is biased toward collecting confirmatory evidence), which in turn strengthens our current beliefs. However, relying solely upon this style of inquiry is problematic and can lead the individual to a false conclusion because they do not seek out discrediting evidence to complement the confirmatory evidence. Critical thinking, however, demands that we seek out all the evidence, not simply one side, but we as individual critical thinkers operate with a cognitive system that is biased toward confirmatory evidence.

An early study investigating confirmation bias in the laboratory was conducted by Peter Wason (1960). In this study, twenty-nine psychology undergraduates were given the following instructions:

> You will be given three numbers which conform to a simple rule that I have in mind. This rule is concerned with a relation between any three numbers and not with their absolute magnitude, i.e. it is not a rule like all numbers above (or below) 50, etc.
>
> Your aim is to discover this rule by writing down sets of three numbers, together with reasons for your choice of them. After you have written down each set, I shall tell you whether your numbers conform to the rule or not, and you can make a note of this outcome on the record sheet provided. There is no time limit but you should try to discover this rule by citing the minimum sets of numbers.
>
> Remember that your aim is not simply to find numbers which conform to the rule, but to discover the rule itself. When you feel highly confident that you have discovered it, *and not before*, you are to write it down and tell me what it is. Have you any questions? (131)

On the answer sheet, participants were given the numbers 2-4-6. The experiment ended if the participant wrote down the correct rule but continued until the participant found the correct rule, wished to end the experiment, or exceeded forty-five minutes (only six of the twenty-nine participants obtained the correct rule after the first announcement). This task was chosen because there are an unlimited number of sets of numbers that are consistent with the rule of *"three numbers in increasing order of magnitude"* (130). Thus, relying solely upon confirmatory strategies is problematic. What Wason found was that when people misidentified the pattern (i.e., formed a false belief about the rule), they relied upon a strategy of searching for evidence to confirm a belief they had constructed (e.g., giving the numbers 12,

14, 16 to test the belief that the rule was counting by twos). In contrast, strategies to disconfirm the belief, which in this instance is easily done (e.g., giving the numbers 12, 17, 25 to disconfirm the counting by twos), typically is not initially done but is the more effective strategy in this circumstance (by the end of the task, twenty-one out of the twenty-nine students were able to identify the rule).

Wason's study provided empirical evidence that we are biased toward initially seeking evidence to verify our theories about the world, as opposed to seeking to disprove our beliefs. However, in the natural setting, unlike in this study, there is no experimenter providing the individual with feedback about whether or not our beliefs are correct. Thus, in everyday life, (a) we are not given feedback that confirmatory strategies alone are problematic and do not always lead to the correct answer, and (b) we can add "evidence" to confirm our misguided beliefs.

In addition, confirmation bias has been demonstrated in a wide variety of contexts. People tend to seek out and favor information that is consistent with social stereotypes and political beliefs (Johnston 1996). For example, one well-known stereotype is that of the "dumb blonde." For those that believe the stereotype, the bias is toward seeking out evidence that is consistent with the belief (i.e., a blonde entertainer not knowing if tuna, labeled "Chicken of the Sea," is actually poultry or fish). However, they will not actively seek out disconfirming evidence, such as identifying very intelligent blondes. Likewise, political beliefs lead people to seek out information and publications that are consistent with existing views (e.g., the *New York Times* and the *Wall Street Journal* have different readerships). Those who read such publications as *Skeptic* and *Skeptical Inquirer* differ in their beliefs in comparison to those who read psychical or New Age–friendly publications. The important issue, however, is that because of the bias toward gathering confirmatory evidence, the belief becomes strengthened and ultimately more resistant to change (i.e., blondes really are dumb if you only seek confirmatory evidence of that claim; of course, brunettes and redheads would also fall into that category using this strategy).

Research has shown that financial decisions are influenced by the confirmation bias (Schulz-Hardt, Frey, Lüthgens, and Moscovici 2000). The confirmation bias also plays an important role for the hypochondriac, as normal signals from the body are interpreted as confirmatory evidence of one type of illness or another (Pennebaker and Skelton 1978). Interestingly, the work of Swann (1997) indicates that people will select partners who will confirm their own views of themselves. Specifically, people with positive self-views seek relationships with those that view them positively, while people with negative self-views seek partners that provide unfavorable feedback. In a related phenomenon (i.e., another indication of a biased cognitive system), research also indicates that people are more willing to accept desirable as compared with undesirable information (Ditto and Lopez 1992). Specifically, unfavorable medical tests result in much more skepticism than favorable medical tests (i.e., how often does a person ask for a second opinion when receiving good news from the doctor even though there may have been a missed diagnosis of a real problem?). Of course, skeptics are well aware of the confirmation bias that exists among believers in psychic phenomena. One psychic prediction that comes true is latched onto (i.e., confirmatory evidence), while a thousand misses are not actively sought out. Natural selection, however, has resulted in all of us having this bias to confirm what we already believe.

Finally, let's look at the example of the individual who has developed a belief that he would be happier without his current spouse and is considering the possibility of asking for a divorce. Typically, the person will confirm the belief by seeking out and noticing all of the flaws and weaknesses of his partner (e.g., my spouse is selfish, my spouse nags me, my spouse does not help enough around the house, my spouse does not spend enough time with the children, my spouse is cheap, and so forth). Of course, since every individual has flaws and weaknesses, finding confirmatory evidence is not hard. However, in this circumstance, individuals do not typically seek out evidence of how their spouse currently contributes to their lives and how their life may be unhappier without their current spouse. Simply put, we ignore the good points and strengths of our spouse while actively seeking out and focusing only on the bad points (Glenn 1991). Interestingly, many people (certainly not all, as some relationships are so dysfunctional that divorce is a relief) after initiating and going through with a divorce find themselves regretting the decision, likely because their evaluation of the evidence was biased (i.e., they did not consider both the confirmatory and disconfirmatory evidence).

The importance of the confirmation bias is that it generates additional collateral evidence that reinforces and strengthens the belief, making it more resistant to the influence of discrediting information. Furthermore, the belief can persist even when the initial evidence is discredited because people can draw on evidence obtained from a variety of sources. For example, let's say a football fan takes his family to the local zoo on a Saturday afternoon. While at the zoo, he notices the lion letting out a series of ferocious roars. The next day, when checking the football scores, he notices that the Detroit Lions, perennial underdogs in the game, won quite easily. A belief is developed that animals can give signals about subsequent sporting events. Of course, it is not hard to find more confirmatory evidence (e.g., your fish dies and that week the Miami Dolphins lose) while not actively seeking out disconfirming evidence and ignoring inconsistent evidence (e.g., your cat is sick, but the Carolina Panthers still win). By the time you visit the zoo the following year, the belief now has a variety of sources supporting it. Thus, if the lion roars this year, the belief will persist even if the Lions lose on Sunday.

I am hoping that at this point in the discussion the reader is wondering if the confirmation bias has been demonstrated in individuals who have been trained to think critically. This is an important issue, because this book hypothesizes that we as critical thinkers are also prone to the same biases that can mislead us in the same contexts as everyone else because the biases are part of our evolutionary heritage. Unfortunately, there is no record of research performed specifically with critical thinkers, but there is recorded research performed with scientists (i.e., individuals trained in the scientific method and many of whom are critical thinkers). So, any predictions on whether or not scientists typically show the confirmation bias?

Remember the study conducted by Peter Wason in which students were attempting to identify a simple mathematical rule? Mahoney and DeMonbreun (1977) used the same procedures, except the time limit was reduced to ten minutes, and compared fifteen PhD physical scientists (engineers and physicists), fifteen PhD academic psychologists (trained in the scientific method), and fifteen conservative religious ministers (education level ranged from high school through a bachelor's degree). Just like the psychology undergraduate students, participants relied primarily upon confirmatory strategies: over half in each group never disconfirmed, and 93 percent of the physical scientists and psychologists reconfirmed a previously falsified hypothesis compared with 53 percent of the ministers. Results showed no statistical differences between the groups in eventually obtaining the correct hypothesis: 27 percent of the physical scientists, 47 percent of the psychologists, and 40 percent of the ministers.

Although we need to treat a single small-sample study with caution, one interesting finding was "that the scientists in this study appeared to be strongly inclined toward early speculation with relatively little experimentation" (Mahoney and DeMonbreun 1977, 237). Specifically, the average number of experiments prior to announcing their first hypothesis was 1.93 for the psychologists, 1.07 for the physical scientists, and 5.40 for the ministers. Once again, caution is in order. However, this study provides no evidence that those trained in the scientific method (both the physical scientists and psychologists) possess any superior ability to control the confirmation bias.

There is a large literature consistent with the interpretation that humans have a built-in bias of verifying, as opposed to falsifying, our beliefs. As a quick test of the confirmation bias, I challenge the reader to quickly browse through your personal collection of books. Do you have an equal number of books that are inconsistent with your beliefs as those that are consistent, or are the majority consistent? At least in my case (glancing over at the bookshelves), I am guilty of the confirmation bias when it comes to the books in my personal collection, even on topics that are inherently ambiguous and where widespread disagreement exists even among the brightest scholars.

To summarize: in politics, in love relations, and in a wide variety of real-world contexts, the psychological literature clearly indicates that it is a human response to search for evidence to support what is already believed, while failing to search with equal vigor for evidence that will discredit our beliefs. There currently exists no evidence that scientists, who have been trained in the scientific method (and are the closest group to critical thinkers that I could find for comparison), control this bias. This bias, however, has the evolutionary advantage of making our accurate beliefs more resistant to change, as we add evidence to bolster the beliefs (i.e., increase our confidence). Of course, the trade-off is that it also results in making our inaccurate beliefs more resistant to change as well.

Biased Assimilation

Prior to reviewing some of the pertinent literature on this topic, I hope the reader will indulge me in a quick anecdotal story, which is supported by the literature below. When teaching in the classroom, I typically wear dress pants, a dress shirt, a tie, and shoes. Thus, the preconceived notion my students have of me is that I wear dress clothes to work, and they can easily identify me under conditions consistent with their preconceived notion. For example, when I see students in the hallways on days that I teach, I will say "hi" and they typically respond with an appropriate greeting. What is interesting is when I come to campus on days that I do not teach. I typically wear jeans, sneakers, and so on (i.e., a casual look that is inconsistent with their preconceived notion). Of course, I will still say "hi" to my students on these days when I pass them in the hallways. However, I cannot tell the reader how many times I have been given a puzzled look (i.e., who is this guy?) instead of the usual returned greeting. I have asked students about this later (when wearing dress clothes), and the one consistent answer I receive is "That was you?" In essence, the preconceived notion (Riniolo wears dress clothes) interfered with the ability to evaluate evidence (who is that guy saying "hi" to me?).

Not only do we possess a bias toward gathering evidence already consistent with our current beliefs, but current beliefs (i.e., preconceived notions) directly influence our ability to objectively and critically analyze evidence (i.e., biased assimilation). In one study (Rothbart and Birrell 1977), the researchers manipulated preconceptions and subsequently the ability of subjects to objectively analyze evidence. Specifically, subjects were required to evaluate the "attributes" of faces in photos as having either a cruel or kind expression. The photos were chosen because they were ambiguous and could reasonably be associated with either an unfavorable or favorable personality. Furthermore, prior to the subjects making their evaluations, character descriptions were prepared, giving the photos either a strong positive or negative bias. Specifically, the pictures were given a biographical sketch describing the person as "a German who either strongly supported or strongly opposed the genocidal policies of Hitler" (210). Likewise, a second biographical sketch described the individual in the photos as either an individual who was self-sacrificing and devoted to helping the poor or who believed the poor were socially and intellectually inferior to others. Predictability, the manipulated preconception—the person in the photograph described as either a wicked or a noble person—altered the judgments of the subjects that evaluated the photographs.

Keep in mind that critical thinking requires an objective analysis of evidence. In this example, the photos should not have been rated as cruel or kind but as ambiguous. However, our preconceived notions interfere with our ability to objectively evaluate uncertain evidence. This ultimately results in our beliefs influencing our objectivity and can result in double standards being applied to the evaluation of evidence. In this instance, the character descriptions, which served to create preconceived notions, biased the evaluation of the evidence. From an evolutionary perspective, this once again has the benefit of biasing us toward strengthening and maintaining beliefs, as even unclear evidence is interpreted as supporting our current beliefs, which ultimately makes them more resistant to change and more likely to be acted upon.

In another example, Darley and Gross (1983) demonstrated how our preconceived notions (i.e., a stereotype) can influence our evaluations. Specifically, seventy undergraduate students viewed a videotape of a female fourth-grader. Half of the subjects viewed a sequence that showed the student in a middle-class suburban environment, while the other half viewed the student in a low-income urban environment. The preconceived notion the researchers were testing was that children from low-income schools are poorer students than children from middle-class backgrounds. Subsequently, participants from both groups were shown the same additional video of the student responding to achievement test problems, which gave no real information about the child's actual abilities. Results from the experiment demonstrated that when the student (the same child for both conditions) was believed to come from a low-income background, her abilities were rated as below average. In contrast, she was rated as well above average by those who believed she came from a middle-class background. Once again, this study indicates that prior beliefs influence our ability to objectively evaluate information. Critical thinking requires objectivity, but all individuals possess biases that interfere with an impartial appraisal.

These types of studies are important for the following reason: even ambiguous data (i.e., data that provides neither confirmatory nor discrediting evidence) is interpreted as confirmatory. Thus, beliefs are strengthened even in the absence of confirmatory evidence because we interpret information within a framework of preexisting beliefs. As a real-world example, the individual who believes in a racial or ethnic stereotype, such as that group is lazy, that group is cheap, or that group has ties to organized crime, will process any new information within a cognitive system that is biased toward the stereotype. Thus, an "average tip" (neither small nor large) left by a person from a specific ethnic group stereotyped as cheap for a waiter is not interpreted objectively but typically reinforces the stereotype (what a cheapskate), which is one of the reasons so many stereotypes persist without supporting evidence. Of course, the same tip left by another individual can be interpreted in a different way (see Hamilton and Rose 1980; Slusher and Anderson 1987; Trolier and Hamilton 1986).

Not surprisingly, strongly held beliefs also bias our ability to objectively evaluate evidence. In one study, Lord, Ross, and Lepper (1979) used subjects who had strong beliefs about the deterrent effect of capital punishment on potential murderers. One group believed capital punishment is an effective deterrent, while the other group believed it an ineffective deterrent. Subsequently, both groups were given what they believed were two genuine studies on the effectiveness of capital punishment as a deterrent. Results indicated that prior beliefs determined how subjects rated the quality of the two studies they reviewed. Furthermore, subject's beliefs on the topic became more confident after reading both reports. As the authors noted, "People who hold strong opinions on complex social issues are likely to examine relevant empirical evidence in a biased manner. They are apt to accept 'confirming' evidence at face value while subjecting 'disconfirming' evidence to critical evaluation and as a result to draw undue support for their initial positions from mixed or random empirical findings" (Lord, Ross, and Lepper 1979, 2098). Many similar studies have found consistent results; however, critical thinking requires that all evidence is subjected to an objective evaluation.

Of course, it's one thing for research subjects (typically college students) to have their preconceived notions influence their ability to objectively evaluate evidence, but do those who are trained to be dispassionate observers, such as researchers who referee manuscripts for scientific journals, overcome this shortcoming? Unfortunately, the evidence shows just the opposite (Bornstein 1990; Hojat, Gonnella, and Caelleigh 2003; Mahoney 1985, 1987). As one example, Mahoney (1977) sent manuscripts with identical introductions and experimental procedures (no discussion section) to seventy-five journal reviewers. The manuscripts varied the results of the experiment. Interestingly, "reviewers were strongly biased against manuscripts which reported results contrary to their theoretical perspective" (161). More disturbing, the experimental procedures were treated as vastly different, either excellent or poor, based upon the preconceived notions of the reviewers. As Myers (2005, 101) nicely articulates, "One reason our beliefs are so important; they shape our interpretation of everything else." A large literature supports this assertion, and even those trained to implement the scientific method have not been demonstrated to be immune from the influence of personal beliefs. Finally, for those interested in further reading on how our thoughts and beliefs can shape our interpretations of the world, Thomas Sowell's (2002) *A Conflict of Visions* is highly recommended.

Belief Perseverance

Research has also demonstrated that in some circumstances it can be very difficult to change a belief even when substantial discrediting information is provided. Psychologists call this belief perseverance. This is especially true when an individual has constructed a rationale supporting the belief. Let's review a few (there are many more) studies on this issue (see Jelalian and Miller 1984 for a review of the early literature). In one study (Anderson and Kellam 1992), subjects were asked to consider the following question: Does a risk-prone person or a cautious person make a better firefighter? In this study, subjects were asked to write an explanation to support their opinions. Of course, a rationale for each is theoretically justified (i.e., the risk taker is more likely to rescue people from burning buildings; the cautious individual is more likely not to make rash decisions in a dangerous situation). Interestingly, after the subjects formed their rationale (i.e., developed an explanation for their beliefs), when provided with discrediting information, subjects continued to hang onto their beliefs. In essence, once beliefs are formed, we become resistant to information that is inconsistent with them. Please note that this does not mean that we cannot change our beliefs (that, of course, can and does occur), but the evidence clearly indicates we are biased toward maintaining them. There likely exists substantial individual differences based upon the individual, the amount of evidence supporting the belief, and the specific beliefs being challenged.

My personal favorite study investigating this issue of belief perseverance was conducted by Lepper, Ross, and Lau (1986). In this study, high school students were shown either a highly effective teaching video clip instructing them on how to solve complex problems (i.e., a success condition) or a highly ineffective teaching video that did not show them how to solve the complex problems (i.e., a failure condition). The success-condition students developed beliefs that they were highly competent, while those in the failure condition believed themselves to be incompetent and likely not to benefit from further instruction. The interesting portion of the experiment came after the beliefs were formed. Specifically, both groups were shown the other teaching video (i.e., a plausible alternative explanation for success or failure was given). However, despite the fact that students are aware that good teachers can help students learn, and poor teachers can contribute to a student not being able to master material, the students' beliefs about themselves (i.e., competent or incompetent) persisted. As the authors note, their results suggest that "the perseverance of discredited initial beliefs may occur even when subjects are demonstrably aware of the fact that their performance had been determined largely by a factor other than their own ability at the task" (489). Simply put, a bias exists toward maintaining our established beliefs, even our false beliefs.

Of course, we as critical thinkers are all too familiar with belief perseverance when dealing with a "true believer" in psychic phenomena. I personally made the mistake of trying to convince a true believer that the "psychic" demonstration they had witnessed was likely just a simple magic trick (e.g., spoon bending). I even went so far as to demonstrate how spoon bending was performed. I should have known better, because the discussion ended an hour later, with both of us equally frustrated with the other. Yet, nothing I could say or do could convince him (I'm sure he felt the same way about me) of the possibility that he only saw a magic trick, not a true psychic occurrence.

A few years back, several students and I (see Riniolo, Koledin, Drakulic, and Payne 2003) performed research that provides a nice example of the bias toward maintaining beliefs. The research was centered on the accuracy of eyewitness testimony obtained from archives from *Titanic* survivors about the ship's final plunge (the United States Senate and British Board of Trade hearings from 1912 are available at http://www.titanicinquiry.org/). Specifically, we were interested in determining whether the witnesses recalled the ship as "breaking" or as being "intact" during the final plunge. With the discovery of the *Titanic* in 1985, it was subsequently possible to perform a forensic analysis that indicated there was "no doubt" (Garzke, Brown, Sandiford, Woodward, and Hsu 1996, 250) that the ship was breaking apart as it sank. Thus, it was now possible to quantify the accuracy of the eyewitness testimony on this specific aspect of the tragedy because there is a known outcome (i.e., the ship was breaking). We identified twenty eyewitnesses who directly commented on this issue, and of them, 75 percent testified that the ship had been breaking.

What is important for the current discussion is that both the US Senate and British Board of Trade concluded that the *Titanic* sank intact. Furthermore, *Titanic* historians, and virtually every author writing about the *Titanic*, concluded the ship sank intact prior to 1985. Eva Hart, who witnessed the tragedy when she was only seven years old (her father died that night), had been repeatedly told by experts that her memory of the ship's final plunge was wrong, as she insisted over the years that *Titanic* had been breaking (she never wavered from her position).

The interesting question is why did virtually all of the evaluators ignore the only evidence (75 percent of the eyewitnesses said breaking apart) available to them at the time? Our interpretation was "that the evaluators had a preexisting bias to interpret the tragedy in the best possible light" (93). Note that it was a widely held belief at the time the *Titanic* sailed that it was "the most perfect work of naval architecture the world had ever produced" (Wood 1912, 160). Thus, the preexisting belief in the "unsinkable" ship influenced the evaluators toward belief maintenance, despite the fact that the *Titanic* had just demonstrated it clearly was not unsinkable. Thus, if the ship did sink, it must have been intact (that is closer to the initial belief than the ship crumbling apart).

Once again, the issue of whether or not those trained in the scientific method are likely to overcome this bias should be addressed. Simply put, the answer is no. In fact, one might argue that those of us who spend decades seeking confirmatory evidence to support our beliefs, such as scientists and critical thinkers, are most resistant to change our beliefs because we have developed an enormous structure of supporting evidence. Unfortunately, the "ideal" notion of the dispassionate scientist who is influenced by data and is always open to the possibility of new discoveries often does not match reality (see Mahoney 1976; Mitroff 1974, 1974a; Sagan 1996). This helps to explain why in science a new theory (e.g., plate tectonics) is often not accepted within the scientific community until the current generation of scientists is replaced by the next generation.

The work of Ian Mitroff (1974) on this topic is most illuminating. Specifically, Mitroff intensively interviewed forty-two prestigious scientists (Nobel Prize winners were included in this group) who would eventually study the lunar rocks before the lunar landing of Apollo 11, 12, 14, and 15. These scientists were the best of the best. One of the reasons Mitroff chose the Apollo moon scientists was:

> A major initial premise (later confirmed) was that the Apollo program would be an excellent contemporary setting in which to study the nature and function of the commitment of scientists to their pet hypotheses in the face of possibly disconfirming evidence. A review of the scientific and popular literature before the landing of Apollo 11 found that various scientists had strongly committed themselves in print as to what they thought the moon would be like, and in a few cases, what they ardently hoped the moon would be like. (581)

Mitroff's interviews demonstrated that the scientists typically refused to alter their beliefs in response to new evidence (i.e., actual moon rocks), and recognized this characteristic in their peers. The following is a composite sketch of the three most dogmatic scientists, who were also judged as three of the most outstanding in this group of already elite scientists:

> X is so committed to the idea that the moon is Q that you could literally take the moon apart piece by piece, ship it back to Earth, reassemble it in X's backyard and shove the whole thing . . . and X

would still continue to believe that the moon is Q. X's belief in Q is unshakeable. He refuses to listen to reason or to evidence. (586)

Most fascinating, Mitroff notes that the composite did not change at all during the three and a half years of the study. In essence, irrefutable data, in some instances, is not enough to shake the beliefs of those trained in the scientific method. For those interested in a more detailed account, see Mitroff's (1974a) *The Subjective Side of Science*. Once again, specific research has not been conducted with critical thinkers, but I have no reason to suspect we would be immune from the biases displayed by everyone else, as we are not exempt from our evolutionary heritage (once again, I refer the reader to the illusion in chapter 5).

Finally, the research of Philip Tetlock (1998, 1999) provides some fascinating insight into the belief systems of experts. If anyone should be able to overcome our evolutionary biases, perhaps it is experts, because experts typically possess self-monitoring skills. Specifically, Tetlock has been collecting expert opinions about the future of various economic, political, and military outcomes. For example, he has had experts predict the future of the Soviet Union in 1988 and the future of Canada and South Africa in 1992. In the Soviet Union, experts were asked if they were predicting "a strengthening, a reduction, or no change in Communist Party control" (648). Experts were then asked to reflect on their predictions at both five- and ten-year intervals. This research is important not only for documenting the accuracy rates of experts, but it allowed an investigation of how the experts responded when confirming or disconfirming evidence occurred.

Interestingly, those experts who made predictions that were wrong had as much confidence in their opinions as those experts who accurately predicted the future. Most important for this discussion is that while some experts (a minority) used disconfirming evidence to moderate their views, many experts implemented cognitive strategies to "bolster their beliefs systems, both by protecting prior understandings of the past and by cushioning conditional forecasts from refutation" (651). Three such strategies that experts, who were flat-out wrong, used to maintain belief systems included close-call counter-factuals (their predicted outcome almost occurred; "The hardliners almost succeeded in their coup attempt against Gorbachev"), off/on timing (the predicted outcome will occur in the future; communism will return), and trivializing failure (specific political events are inherently unpredictable; it's just a guessing game). Thus, experts will also go to great lengths to maintain belief systems, even in the face of strong evidence that should have forced them to reconsider their belief system in response to the outcomes that occurred. Yet, this is predictable because of the evolutionary bias toward maintaining beliefs, which is interconnected with our pattern-seeking heritage.

SUMMARY

This chapter theorized that our pattern-seeking tendencies provide a greater evolutionary advantage when complemented by a cognitive system that is biased toward strengthening and maintaining beliefs. This chapter has documented several of the important biases that we all possess, which ultimately can interfere with our ability to think critically and objectively evaluate claims in certain situations based upon our own individual beliefs. However, even if the evolutionary explanation that is offered is wrong and our pattern-seeking heritage is not interconnected with our cognitive biases (placing things within an evolutionary context can be a speculative venture at times), it does not change the fact that humans have a biased cognitive system designed to maintain and strengthen all beliefs, even those that are false. Our biased cognitive system contributes to us all being inconsistent critical thinkers in some situations because we all are influenced by our current beliefs. An awareness of that simple fact is a necessary first step in identifying and limiting our own biases from interfering with our ability to evaluate claims in certain situations.

Finally, the reader may be wondering which came first, the pattern-seeking or the biases towards strengthening and maintaining beliefs. Within an evolutionary framework, plausible rationales can be made that would theorize that pattern-seeking preceded, developed simultaneously, or followed the development of our biased cognitive system. I do not wish at this point to even venture a guess. The important issue for this book is not which came first (the chicken or the egg), but that at some point in our struggle for survival, pattern-seeking and our biased cognitive system became interconnected, which provided an overall benefit. This ultimately contributed to both persisting in us today.

Chapter 8

THE ROLE OF EMOTIONS IN BELIEF MAINTENANCE

I would warn the critic, however, not to be led away by the sophistry that because some professional trickster, apt at the game of deception, can produce a somewhat similar effect, therefore the originals were produced in the same way.
—Sir Arthur Conan Doyle, *The Coming of the Fairies* (1922, 3),
discussing the authenticity of the Cottingley fairy photographs

Have you ever been "passionately" in love with someone (e.g., high school sweethearts)? Have you ever been so angry that you could feel yourself losing control (e.g., a divorcing couple in the midst of a bitter custody dispute)? Have you ever been so scared that you lost physical control of your bodily functions and froze, unable to move (e.g., an intruder has broken into your house during the middle of the night and puts a knife to your throat)? Have you ever felt such intense happiness that you were on top of the world (e.g., a die-hard sports fan whose team finally wins the championship; as a Buffalo native, I have yet to experience this feeling, but hope springs eternal!)? Have you ever experienced such intense grief that it hurt at the gut level (e.g., parents losing a child in a drinking and driving accident)? If you have ever experienced any of these feelings, you have experienced an intense emotional response.

From an evolutionary perspective, the role of emotions is to automatically help an individual respond correctly to universal situations in which the appropriate response will increase the chances of either survival or reproduction. Let's take, for example, the universal situation of predator/prey. Imagine the prey, a bunny rabbit is hopping along, and from behind a tree leaps the predator, a wolf. The role of emotions is to trigger the automatic emotional response of fear in the rabbit, which leads to the appropriate behavioral response of running away. Note in this scenario, the rabbit has a good chance of survival because the emotional response triggers the appropriate behavioral action. Could you imagine the fate of the rabbit if it showed a different emotional response (e.g., fell in love or got angry with the wolf), or was simply indifferent to the wolf's presence? In all likelihood, that rabbit would end its days as a nice lunch for the predator.

Intense emotional responses are typically processed in the portion of the brain known as the limbic system. The limbic system, which is involved in controlling the body's hormones, is an older neural system that is involved in a variety of functions such as memory, drives (e.g., sex, food), and emotional responses. As an example, if you have ever seen a really angry cat (e.g., arched back, claws out, fur standing up, hissing), that cat is showing a limbic-driven response (specifically involving the amygdala, which influences aggression and fear responses). Also, those "passionately" in love teenage couples who can't stop thinking about each other and rush back to their lockers in between classes so they can make out for a few minutes are likewise showing emotional responses driven by the limbic system.

What is important to consider here, however, is the role of emotional responses in influencing our ability to accurately evaluate information. For example, is the passionately in love couple able to accurately evaluate the "strengths" and "weaknesses" their partner possesses while processing information from this older neural system? The answer is typically no, because our ability to critically analyze information (i.e., see our partners in a realistic light) is processed in the frontal lobes, not the limbic system. What is interesting about the "love" example is that passionate love does not continue indefinitely.

I like to think of passionate love as a cloud in your brain that limits your ability to see the weaknesses in your partner while subsequently magnifying their strengths. It is an interesting experience for some, once the cloud dissipates (i.e., the processing of information shifts from the limbic system to the frontal lobes), to have a more realistic picture of what their partner is really like (some are pleased, while others wonder what they could have possibly been thinking!). Simply put, emotions can influence our ability to accurately evaluate information. (As another example, attend a youth sporting event and try to determine if the emotional attachments that parents have to their children interfere with their ability to accurately evaluate the talent level of their child's ability to play soccer or baseball.)

Although this book focuses upon the cognitive biases that make us prone to maintain our beliefs and be inconsistent critical thinkers, the influence of emotions on our beliefs cannot be ignored. Research indicates that when beliefs were formed based primarily upon emotional input, those beliefs were subsequently more resistant to cognitive persuasion and logical arguments (Edwards 1990; Fabrigar and Petty 1999), perhaps because the beliefs were formed based upon substantial input from the limbic system. In any case, emotional beliefs are also resistant to discrediting information. For example, imagine that you take a trip to the pet store to purchase a new pet for your family (you have a spouse, a young child, and live in the city). While looking at all of the potential pets, you absolutely "fall in love" with a puppy (i.e., an emotional belief that this is the right pet for your family is formed). Let's be honest here, some dogs have temperaments that would make a much better fit for a city family with a young infant than others. Simply put, once an emotionally based belief is formed (i.e., that's the dog for me), it will be much more difficult to change the belief (i.e., information by the store clerk that that breed of dog would be much happier living in the country and is not the best choice to be around an infant).

EXAMPLES OF EMOTIONS INFLUENCING
OBJECTIVE EVALUATION

Sir Arthur Conan Doyle

Perhaps there is no other character in the history of literature better known for his logical reasoning, deductive skills, critical thinking, and ability to sift through the evidence to discover the truth than Sherlock Holmes. Interestingly, Sir Arthur Conan Doyle, the author of the Sherlock Holmes mysteries, provides an example of how a great mind can be misguided and how, once a belief is formed (especially an emotionally based belief), evidence is evaluated within our cognitive systems that is biased toward maintaining beliefs.

Prior to discussing the specific issues related to Conan Doyle, a little background information is necessary to put the event in its proper context. Modern spiritualism, whose central claim is that special individuals could communicate with the spirits of the dead, began on March 31, 1848, in Hydesville, New York (just outside of Rochester), at the Fox farm. Margaret and Kate Fox (conflicting accounts of the exact age of the sisters have been reported in various sources, but they were approximately eleven and nine years old, respectively) pulled a childhood prank on their mother. The sisters initially used an apple tied to a string and bounced it off of the floor to produce "rapping noises." (They later learned that they could make rapping noises by cracking their toe joints.) They deceived their mother into believing a spirit was present and could communicate through them.

This childhood prank quickly got out of hand. As Margaret Fox Kane wrote in her confession many years later (originally published in the *New York World* on October 21, 1888), it started "as a mere trick to frighten mother, and then, when so many people came to see us children, we were frightened ourselves and kept it up" (Fox Kane 1985, 227). The girls' older sister, who saw the money-making potential, took her sisters to Rochester, where they communicated with the loved ones of paying customers. Prior to 1888, when the sisters confessed they were frauds and explained how they produced the rapping noises, the Fox sisters were international celebrities who had performed séances for Queen Victoria in England and at the White House. With the massive amount of life lost from the Civil War, many grieving people were willing to pay for the chance to communicate once again with loved ones (and many mediums quickly sprang up to take the money from paying customers).

After the "rappings" lost their initial appeal, mediums turned to more complex forms of communication in the darkened séance room. For example, mediums produced spirit messages on slate boards, spirit voices would transmit messages through megaphones, spirit photography would capture the spirits on film, physical manifestations of the spirits (such as ectoplasm) would occur, and automatic writing (the spirit allegedly transmitted a written message through the medium), and so forth. However, by the late 1800s, interest in spiritualism diminished, likely because of the Fox sisters' confession, combined with many of the other famous mediums of the time being exposed as frauds. However, with the massive losses of life that subsequently occurred from World War I, spiritualism had a resurgence in 1918, especially in Europe where the war casualties were the greatest.

Conan Doyle himself, like many people at the time, had been interested in the supernatural. However, a turning point occurred when his son Kingsley died during World War I. Like many who had lost sons, brothers, and husbands during this time, Conan Doyle turned to spiritualism as a way to cope with grief that accompanies the death of a loved one (i.e., an emotionally based belief influenced by the grief that accompanies the loss of a child). Likewise, his second wife, Jean, subsequently lost her brother to the war and not only became committed to spiritualism but became a medium herself and communicated with the spirits using automatic writing. From that point on, the Conan Doyles became great champions of not only the spiritualist movement but any related supernatural claims.

To keep things in context, it should be noted that Conan Doyle was not alone in his support of the spiritualist hypothesis (i.e., the mediums were legitimately communicating with spirits as opposed to being clever conjurers or deceiving themselves and their clients). Other men of science who held the same beliefs as Conan Doyle included the naturalist Alfred Russel Wallace (cofounder of the theory of natural selection); physicists Sir Oliver Lodge, Sir William Crookes, Lord Rayleigh; psychologists William James (still considered one of the greatest American psychologists) and William McDougall; the French biologist Charles Richet; philosopher Hans Driesch, to name some of the more prominent supporters. Thus, while it is easy to look back with the benefit of hindsight, many prominent individuals had believed in this phenomenon.

Prior to discussing the most apparent example of Conan Doyle's inconsistent critical thinking, his curious friendship with Harry Houdini provides additional useful information (see Polidoro 2001, *Final Séance*, 2001, for further information). Houdini, who had previously performed as a medium himself, had a deep interest in spiritualism dating back to a visit to a medium after his father died when Houdini was eighteen. Houdini and Conan Doyle first met in 1919 when Houdini was performing in Brighton, England. Of course, when Houdini, a master conjurer, observed mediums perform, he could quickly observe the trickery that was occurring. Later on, Houdini made it a point to expose mediums as frauds (although he was always open to the possibility of communication with the dead and personally made compacts with fourteen individuals that whomever died first would attempt to contact the other). The exposing of the conjuring techniques used by mediums resulted in Houdini's book, *Houdini: A Magician among the Spirits* (1924/1972), which is required reading for those who want detailed information about how mediums performed their feats early in the twentieth century. A more recent example is Keene's *The Psychic Mafia* (1997), which is also a must-read.

Houdini provides insight into the mind and biases of Conan Doyle. First, Houdini (1924/1972) describes Conan Doyle in the following way, "He is a brilliant man, a deep thinker, well versed in every respect" (138). However, when it comes to spiritualism, he believes only "if it is favorable to Spiritualism" (139). For example, Houdini notes that Sir Arthur "insists that the Fox Sisters were genuine, even though both Margaret and Katie confessed to fraud and explained how and why they became mediums and the methods used by them to produce the raps" (141). Worse yet, despite Houdini being able to explain and show Conan Doyle how mediums perform, "Sir Arthur thinks that I have great mediumistic powers and that some of my feats are done with the aid of spirits" (165). Simply put, when it came to spiritualism, or any type of supernatural phenomena, Sir Arthur went to great lengths to maintain his belief system, likely because of the emotional investment in the beliefs themselves.

One last diversion is necessary, and it provides a historical example of how people with no training in conjuring can be easily fooled by a conjurer. Specifically, Harry Houdini's most famous investigation of a medium was his showdown with "The Blond Witch of Lime Street," Mina Crandon (aka, Margery). Margery had been recommended by Conan Doyle to *Scientific American*, who had recently put together a panel to investigate mediums. The panel included Dr. McDougall (Harvard University), Dr. Comstock (formerly of the Massachusetts Institute of Technology), Dr. Prince (Society for Psychical Research), Hereward Carrington, and Houdini. J. Malcolm Bird (secretary of the committee) and Dr. Lescaboura (assisted in arranging evaluations of mediums) were both members of *Scientific American*'s editorial staff. The magazine was offering a $5,000 prize (the initial prize was $2,500, but there was limited interest) for a demonstration of psychic powers under controlled conditions.

Margery did not have an interest in the money, as she did not charge for her demonstrations, nor did she accept donations or gifts. She had agreed in advance to donate the prize money to psychic research if she claimed the prize. Massimo Polidoro, cofounder of the Italian skeptics group, has a fascinating interview with Margery's great-granddaughter, and the interview provides some insight into Margery's potential motives for being a medium (Polidoro 2002). Likewise, the father of parapsychology, J. B. Rhine, and his wife, Louisa, investigated Margery and concluded she was an outright fraud in an article published in the *Journal of Abnormal and Social Psychology* (Rhine and Rhine 1927). The Rhines also speculate on Margery's motivation to take on the role of the medium. For readers who are interested in a historical perspective as to why females have taken on these types of roles, see Spanos (1994).

Margery, in addition to being the most skilled medium of her time, was also a very beautiful and sexually alluring woman who has not afraid to display her body (usually with little clothing) and use her sexuality to distract during the séance. J. Malcolm Bird and at least one of the committee members, Hereward Carrington, had by all accounts fallen in love with her (i.e., emotions can influence the ability to make accurate judgments). By the summer of 1924, Margery had initially been thoroughly evaluated by various members of the *Scientific American* panel at her Boston home. Her husband, Dr. Crandon, a well-known Boston surgeon, reported that the number of séances for various committee members approximated eighty (Houdini 1924).

The previous evaluations of Margery were performed without Houdini's knowledge. Houdini was outraged as he rightfully believed his reputation was at stake if the committee awarded the prize to a medium who was eventually detected as a fraud. Unfortunately, the panel, with the exception of Houdini, put together to investigate mediums, was no match for the alluring and highly skilled medium. Houdini (1924) would state after his investigation, "I will go on record that it has required my thirty years of experience to actually detect her in her subtle moves" (23). In fact, the July 1924 issue of *Scientific American* contained an article written by Bird hinting that the prize was as good as won. This would have given Margery a stamp of approval from the scientific community, forever cementing her place in history as an "authentic" medium. As an interesting side note, Dr. Crandon had an extensive collection of books explaining how mediums perform their tricks (Houdini 1924, 8).

As previously mentioned, Houdini was outraged to be left out of the testing process, and the showdown between Houdini and Margery (like a boxing match between two undefeated champions) took place during the summer of 1924 with several séances. In the first séances, Houdini determined how Margery may have been performing her tricks. Houdini reported that Margery could make a megaphone appear while having both hands and feet secured by others. He described this as "the '*slickest*' ruse I have ever detected, and it has converted all the skeptics" (Houdini 1924, 8).

In subsequent séances, Houdini had a special cabinet constructed that only had openings for Margery's arms and neck. The showdown includes some controversy. First, during the actual séance, both Margery and Dr. Crandon made it clear that if Houdini saw "the light" (i.e., declared her a genuine medium), they would donate $10,000 to charity. Houdini refused the offer. After Margery was placed in the box (she was required to make a bell ring in front of her), and her arms were securely held by Houdini and Dr. Prince, which negated the chance of any cheating, a spirit channeled through Margery, her brother "Walter," accused Houdini of planting a ruler in the box to discredit Margery. Of course, Houdini accused Margery of smuggling the ruler in as a potential way to cheat. To be fair, it is still unclear who planted the ruler, as various accounts have been given. When Margery became frustrated when no spirit manifestations appeared, the following exchange occurred between Houdini, Margery, and Dr. Comstock (Houdini 1924, 22).

Margery: "I do not believe any medium could manifest under these conditions."

"Well," I replied, "I am not so sure about that. I am not a medium, but still I could allow myself to be stripped nude, searched by your husband who is a surgeon, you control one of my hands and Dr. Crandon the other, and still I could ring the bell or tie knots in handkerchiefs that are on the outside of cabinet box."

"You must possess psychic power then," she answered.

"No," I replied, "I am just a mystifier. Do you care to put me to the test? *I'll do it right now!*"

"That would not prove anything," Dr. Comstock remarked.

"Oh, yes it would," I replied, "it would prove that these things could be accomplished by trickery."

Eventually, Houdini was able to convince all but one member of the committee—Hereward Carrington; Bird was also not convinced—that Margery used trickery by putting on an exposé demonstrating exactly how the tricks were performed. Thus, *Scientific American* and several prominent scientists were saved from making fools of themselves, as Margery was subsequently caught cheating by other investigators (see Prince 1933). Sir Arthur continued to believe that Margery was genuine and extended an invitation to England, which she refused. Readers are referred to *Houdini Exposes the Tricks Used by Boston Medium "Margery"* 1924, and *Margery* (Tietze 1972) for further details on this issue.

With that background information in mind, perhaps no other single event demonstrates that Conan Doyle was influenced by emotionally based beliefs better than the case of the Cottingley fairy photographs. In 1917, two young English girls (Elsie Wright and her cousin Frances Griffith) had taken several "fairy" photographs with Elsie's father's camera. When Elsie's father developed the pictures, he dismissed them as a childhood prank, as they appeared to be obvious fakes (apparently, the Fox sisters are not the only mischievous young girls). However, Elsie's mother eventually took the photographs to a member of the theosophy movement, which believed in such things as fairies, gnomes in the forest, and so forth.

To make a rather long story short (see Randi 1982, or http://www.randi.org/library/cottingley/ for more details and the photos), Conan Doyle became aware of the photographs via a well-known "sensitive," Miss Scatcherd. Conan Doyle was just about to depart on a trip to Australia, so he dispatched a friend to look into this issue and sent the girls a camera to take additional photos. (Perhaps by this time, like with the Fox sisters, the girls were afraid to tell the truth.) Although there were plenty of warning signals that the photos could be fakes (the girls had simply cut out pictures, added wings, and used hatpins stuck into the ground to make the fairies appear to be flying), Conan Doyle chose to ignore evidence that was not consistent with his belief system. Thus, in 1922, Sir Arthur Conan Doyle, the author of the great Sherlock Holmes character, published a book titled *The Coming of the Fairies*, which lays out for the reader evidence about the five fairy photographs taken by the girls in Cottingley. Conan Doyle summarizes the evidence and criticism about the genuineness of the photographs as follows, "[W]hile more evidence will be welcome, there is enough already available to convince any reasonable man that the matter is not one which can be readily dismissed, but that a case actually exists which up to now has not been shaken in the least degree by any of the criticism directed against it" (139).

I would encourage anyone who has the time to read this book (it was reprinted in 2006), if you are interested in a case example of the cognitive and emotional biases that maintain beliefs once formed (i.e., the photos of fairies were legitimate). For those interested in viewing the photographs, you can either use the Internet address listed above, or simply use the key words "Cottingley fairies" in any Internet search engine, as the photographs are widely available.

THE BRITISH SCIENTIFIC COMMUNITY AND PILTDOWN MAN

Charles Darwin's *The Origin of Species* provided the scientific community with a mechanism (i.e., natural selection) to explain evolution. Darwin's subsequent publications (*The Descent of Man, The Expression of the Emotions in Man and Animals*), applied the concept of natural selection and the notion of evolution specifically to humans. Eventually, the scientific community came to accept the notion that man descended from a common ancestor. With this acceptance, the scientific community felt the need to find "the missing link" between man and the highest apes. Likewise, there was some national pride associated with finding fossil remains, as some nations were attempting to claim that the first "true" human evolved within their national borders. For example, Neanderthal skeletons were found in Germany by workmen building a railroad. Likewise, fossils were subsequently found in Spain, Belgium, France, and Java (at that time, a colony of Holland).

Interestingly, the fossil evidence that emerged indicated that our ancient ancestors had humanlike bodies but rather primitive brains. Thus, the fossil evidence indicated that the human body developed first and was only later followed by the development of the large brain. This evidence was contrary to what many had predicted and had hoped to find. Specifically, many scientists at the time were hoping to find that our large brain evolved first, thereby separating us distinctly from other animals. With that in mind, many researchers looking for the "missing link" were hoping to find fossil remains of an extinct being that showed evidence of a humanlike brain combined with a more apelike body.

Unlike many of the other European nations at the time, England could not point to any fossils of significance in the early part of the twentieth century. Thus, England, a country with a rich and proud cultural heritage, had no justifiable evidence that humans developed within its borders. That is, until a humanlike skull, an apelike jaw, and several teeth were found in the Piltdown region of Sussex, England, in 1911 and 1912. The discovery, which would come to be known as Piltdown Man, forced the rewriting of the way human evolution was conceptualized at that point and was consistent with what many scientists were hoping to find. Interestingly, in 1925, Raymond Dart found a fossil in South Africa, the Taung Skull, which he believed at that time belonged to the earliest human ancestor (he would eventually be proven correct). The fossil had a humanlike jaw and a small brain (i.e., did not fit Piltdown), which was inconsistent with what scientists were hoping to find. Moreover, likely because the fossil came from Africa, it was not widely accepted by European scientists. (The widespread hope within the scientific community at the time was that the first humans could not possibly have come from Africa.)

However, not everyone was convinced that Piltdown Man was in fact the missing link. First, the jaw was so apelike, while the skull so humanlike, that some scientists, particularly in the United States and European countries, simply believed that the fossils were not from the same creature. Furthermore, to accept Piltdown Man, one had to discard the significance of the other discoveries. Simply put, Piltdown was inconsistent with the rest of the accumulating fossil record, which indicated a small brain. In contrast, the biggest supporters of the discovery were British scientists, perhaps because Piltdown man provided England with the long sought-after evidence of a human ancestry in England. As Weiner (1955/2003, 12) notes, "By 1915 the British anatomists and palaeontologists were generally of one mind." Rephrased, Piltdown Man was accepted, with few dissenters, despite the ambiguity of the evidence. Additional evidence (e.g., another skull and jaw) came forth over the years. One finding in particular, an odd-looking bone, which many believed looked very much like a cricket bat, was found in Piltdown.

To make a long story short (readers are referred to Weiner's *The Piltdown Forgery* 1955/2003; Walsh's *Unraveling Piltdown* 1996), Piltdown Man was a hoax, perhaps the greatest known hoax in the history of science, as it fooled many both inside and outside of the scientific community. It was determined that the fossils were deliberately stained to give them an older appearance. The apelike jaw, which was likely from an orangutan, had the teeth filed down to give the appearance of humanlike chewing. An initial inspection using a microscope would have revealed that the jaw had been tampered with, but discrediting evidence was not sought out. Modern dating techniques have demonstrated that the skull and jaw, which were believed to be five hundred thousand years old, were much closer to five hundred years old. Likewise, some of the other supporting evidence, the "cricket bat" bone, upon closer inspection, appears to have been carved with a knife. Simply put, there were a variety of potential warning signs that were ignored by the individuals who proclaimed Piltdown to be legitimate (just as there were warning signs that the fairy photographs were forged), but discrediting evidence was either not sought out or was dismissed by those hoping Piltdown Man was truly the missing link.

The one consistent finding, which is important for this chapter, is that those who had the greater emotional investment in Piltdown Man were the least skeptical and had the greatest confidence of the finding both initially and over time. Once again, in this instance, it appears that scientists, who are trained to be dispassionate observers, are also influenced (like others) by their emotional investments in particular beliefs. Finally, the identity of the person who actually started the hoax is one of the great unsolved mysteries in the history of science. Many suspects have been identified (even Sir Arthur Conan Doyle, who may have done so to get back at the scientific community who mocked his views related to the supernatural), but to date, no conclusive evidence has been obtained beyond a reasonable doubt, as there exist several likely candidates. Perhaps, like "Jack the Ripper," Piltdown Man's inventor will remain an unsolved mystery.

Chapter 9
CASE EXAMPLES
An Ordinary Critical Thinker
and a Brilliant Mind

Whenever we study qualitative differences between experiences we are studying mental and not physical events, and much that we believe to know about the external world is, in fact, knowledge about ourselves.
— F. A. Hayek, *The Sensory Order* (1952/1976, pp. 6–7)

It always comes with an impact of surprise to discover that a person who is highly knowledgeable and eminently reasonable in one domain may be an extraordinary fool in other domains.
— Sidney Hook, *Sidney Hook on Pragmatism, Democracy, and Freedom* (2002, p. 98)

THE ORDINARY CRITICAL THINKER

Part II of this book was intended to point out that because of our evolutionary heritage, we all are biased toward strengthening and maintaining current beliefs, both true and false. While this does not mean we cannot change our beliefs (this, of course, can and does occur), we are continually influenced by them and in some instances are prone to be unknowingly inconsistent with our critical thinking in order to bolster and maintain beliefs, even if we possess critical thinking skills.

In order to illustrate these points, I will discuss two case examples of inconsistent critical thinking, one using the beliefs of an ordinary skeptic (myself) and one using the beliefs of an individual with a brilliant mind. In fact, if I were to have you write a list of the ten smartest people to ever walk the face of the earth (and there have been billions and billions), this person is likely to make many people's list. However, let's start with a personal example of my own inconsistent critical thinking, which is extremely discomforting to admit (I feel like I am going on the *Oprah Winfrey Show* to admit some transgression and ask for absolution), especially because as a social scientist I am well aware of our cognitive biases (i.e., our tendencies to look only for confirmatory evidence and to ignore evidence inconsistent with our beliefs). Likewise, as a critical thinker, I know better than to rely upon secondhand sources (my performance did not match my ability in the example that follows). However, my beliefs for years on this topic were based almost exclusively upon a Hollywood movie and did not change until overwhelming evidence was obtained purely by accident; otherwise my beliefs would likely today remain as foolish as they were a few years ago (makes me wonder what other foolish beliefs I currently possess). Interestingly, once I became aware of my silly views, I attributed my new knowledge to my skeptical nature. Of course, it did not occur to me then that for such a long time I had ignored my critical thinking abilities to maintain my beliefs.

Here is the important background information, which may be useful in ascertaining how and why I could have been so foolish (please forgive me!) and hopefully will serve as a model for others not to emulate. First, I believe that Darwin's theory of natural selection is one of the most important theories (if not the most important) in the history of science, and students should be exposed to such an important theory. Thus, I am pro-Darwin and I think that those who do not believe that Darwin's theory should be taught in schools are narrow-minded fools.

With that in mind, I must sheepishly admit that for many years, I believed that the events of the Scopes Monkey Trial, which occurred in the summer of 1925 in Dayton, Tennessee, were accurately captured by the film *Inherit the Wind* (I prefer the 1960 version starring Spencer Tracy, Fredric March, and Gene Kelly; this was also a popular play). Note that I would never accept at face value such films as *The Amityville Horror, The Three Faces of Eve*, or *Erin Brockovich* as accurate portrayals of real events without the benefit of a critical inquiry. As evidenced in chapter 4, I will actively seek out additional information when presented with questionable evidence (e.g., the reports that many repressed memories have been corroborated). Yet here, influenced by my beliefs (Darwin rules! Fundamentalists are fools!), it was easy to accept *Inherit the Wind* without any critical thinking. The film itself portrays the pro-evolutionists (those who believe Darwin should be taught in schools) as the cowboys in white hats (the good guys) and those who wish to banish Darwin from the classroom as a bunch of hypocritical narrow-minded bigots (the bad guys). Why would I question this portrayal, as it fits perfectly in with my view of the world?

To make matters worse, I have a good friend who has specific expertise in church history. For years he had told me that the events surrounding the Monkey Trial were more complicated than presented in the film, and that I should seek out additional evidence. I reasoned that even if the film was not 100 percent accurate, it likely captured the true spirit of the trial. I had no reason to seek out discrediting information and never attempted to do so. To make a long story short, my views about this trial did change, but the change occurred over a long period of time, and I required substantial evidence to alter my beliefs; this ultimately only occurred because I actively sought out information to corroborate my beliefs that the antievolutionary participants in the Scopes trial were fools.

In condensed form, this is what occurred. I obtained a copy of the trial transcripts (see Scopes 1997) with the intent of finding a few selects quotes that would illustrate just what fools those who opposed Darwin's theory actually were. Yes, I was seeking confirmatory evidence. However, as I made my way through the trial notes, I found many instances in which the transcripts (i.e., firsthand materials) differed substantially from *Inherit the Wind*. For example, in the movie, the local community is portrayed as a bunch of hostile, bigoted fools. Yet in the transcripts, both Clarence Darrow (the defense attorney for Scopes) and out-of-town newspaper reporters thank the local community for their kindness and hospitality (see 226, 315). For example, Darrow (226) says, "I came here a perfect stranger and I can say what I have said before that I have not found upon anybody's part—any citizen here in this town or outside, the slightest discourtesy. I have been treated better, kindlier and more hospitably than I fancied would have been the case in the north." However, I reasoned that the movie just took a few liberties but still captured the essence of the trial.

However, many other discrepancies came to my attention (too many to mention here and enough to actually write another book). Note that William Jennings Bryan (called Matthew Harrison Brady in the film), who is part of the prosecution team, is portrayed in the film as a mindless reactionary who never even read Darwin. This is untrue, and from my subsequent inquiry, he appears to be the only lawyer in the case who actually read Darwin's works. During one scene in the film, the defense wanted to call experts to the stand to explain evolution, and Bryan/Brady is portrayed as the narrow-minded fool who objects and keeps the scientists from testifying. Yet in the trial transcripts (see 206), Bryan did not object to the scientists testifying but simply wanted to ensure that he could cross-examine the witnesses (seems fair). It was the defense that refused to put the scientists on the stand, because they did not want a cross-examination. This should have made me wonder why the defense would object to Bryan being able to cross-examine witnesses if he was the mindless reactionary presented in the film. Surely the scientists would have had no trouble in answering his foolish questions. Still, at this point, I did not question the film version.

I could continue with example after example of how the historical record contradicts the film, but it was not until I obtained a copy of Hunter's (1914) *A Civic Biology* (the book that was actually on trial; Darwin's works were not) that I seriously began to question my belief that *Inherit the Wind* accurately portrayed the events of the Monkey Trial. Specifically, in *A Civic Biology*, eugenics (here, forced sterilization of the intellectually and physically "inferior") was portrayed side by side with natural selection as a scientific method to improve humans. For example, the book on trial contained the following information related to eugenics (see 261–63): (a) feeble-mindedness and epilepsy "are handicaps which it is not only unfair but criminal to hand down to posterity," and (b) "If such people were lower animals, we would probably kill them off to prevent them from spreading." Bryan would have grilled the scientists if they did testify on the eugenics issue, which is the likely reason the defense refused to put them on the witness stand. It is important to understand the eugenics issue to put into context why some people did oppose teaching evolution to children at that specific point in history. Of course, *Inherit the Wind* omits that issue from the film. Perhaps one reason I have altered my views on the Monkey Trial is my disgust for the eugenics policies that resulted in widespread sterilizations not only in the United States but in many other countries as well (Riniolo and Torrez 2000).

To make a rather long story short, the Scopes Monkey Trial is not a simple "black and white" event, and my previous beliefs about the trial really are a source of embarrassment. There were many interesting aspects to the trial (the eugenics issue being one of them; how many of us today, besides the village racist, believe that eugenics is appropriate to teach children?) that were omitted from the film. In fact, "the reality of the Monkey Trial barely resembles the fiction of *Inherit the Wind*" (Riniolo and Torrez 2000, 63). I should have known better, but it was easy to accept the fiction because it fit nicely into my worldview, and my critical thinking and skeptical abilities certainly did not make me immune from accepting something that should have been regarded as a careless belief. Once again, if I did not happen to have the time (college professors have their fair share of free time) to read the trial transcripts and subsequently track down a variety of firsthand sources, my views about the trial would likely be as misguided today as they were before, and I would be unaware of these foolish beliefs.

However, this example can be useful in the following way: I am now at least aware of how easy it was for me to abandon my critical thinking skills and to accept information that was uncritically evaluated simply because it was consistent with my beliefs. The challenge is to minimize this happening again and to reevaluate current beliefs that may have been formed in the same uncritical and potentially biased fashion. I wonder with hindsight whether or not my self-identification as a critical thinker led to an overconfidence in my beliefs, as surely I could not believe in nonsense. What a foolish belief that was!

For those interested in further information about the Monkey Trial, I would recommend Larson's (1998) *Summer for the Gods*, which places the trial in the proper historical context and provides an accurate account of the events and people involved in one of the most well-known trials of the twentieth century. Likewise, see Riniolo and Torrez (2000) "Revisiting the Monkey Trial" and Riniolo (2002) "The Attorney and the Shrink," for further relevant information. The first article speculates, using historical records, what Bryan likely would have asked Darrow if he had the opportunity to put him on the witness stand (the most famous aspect of the trial was when Darrow called Bryan to the witness stand as an expert on the Bible). One of the little-known facts about the trial is that Bryan agreed to be grilled by Darrow only if he was in turn allowed to examine all of the defense lawyers, which never happened (Scopes 1997). The second article is a skeptical inquiry into the beliefs of Clarence Darrow, using the same standards that skeptics have applied to Bryan over the years. However, this article focuses on Darrow's involvement in the Leopold and Loeb trial in the summer of 1924, which was, until the O. J. Simpson trial in 1994, the most famous murder trial of the twentieth century and an important event in the history of psychology because the trial introduced the general public to psychoanalysis and Sigmund Freud. These articles were written after I had taken the time to actually perform a critical inquiry (of course, biases are always present) and are perhaps a way to make up for my foolish beliefs. Once again, I'll ask for forgiveness here! For readers who would like copies of the articles, they are available in back issues of *Skeptic* (www.skeptic.com), or feel free to e-mail me at todd.c.riniolo@medaille.edu for a copy.

THE BRILLIANT MIND AND INCONSISTENT CRITICAL THINKING

So, did anyone bother to write down a list of the top ten most brilliant minds? If you are like most people, Albert Einstein was included in your list because of his scientific contributions and his reputation. However, as part of the human species, even someone as brilliant as Einstein is not immune from the cognitive (and emotional) biases that have evolved to strengthen and maintain beliefs once formed, even his most cherished beliefs. (Readers are referred to Riniolo and Nisbet's [2007] recent article "The Myth of Consistent Skepticism: The Cautionary Case of Albert Einstein" in the *Skeptical Inquirer* for additional issues associated with this topic.)

My investigation into the beliefs of Albert Einstein, much like my investigation into the Scopes Trial, also occurred by accident. I had no reason to doubt Einstein's brilliance, as he was an elite scientist and I was unaware of any critical evaluation of his beliefs in the skeptical literature or anywhere else, for that matter. Einstein was voted one of the top ten skeptics of the twentieth century by the Fellows and Scientific Consultants of CSICOP (see *Skeptical Inquirer* Jan/Feb 2000), which provided further evidence that Einstein was not only one of the world's best scientists but an exceptional critical thinker.

One day, I was out of reading materials and drove to the library to pick up some books. I usually like to read (in addition to journal articles and books within my own discipline) topics related to economic issues or history. With that in mind, I was simply browsing through books, when *Stalin: The Glasnost Revelations* by Walter Laqueur (1990) caught my eye. I believed this would be an interesting read because the book was written after the former Soviet Union's new policy of openness but prior to the breakup of the Soviet Union itself. In the chapter "The Cult of Personality," I was surprised to see Einstein's name briefly mentioned as one of the distinguished Western intellectuals who was sympathetic to the Soviet Union during the 1930s. Surely this was either a mistake, as Einstein has a well-known and deserved reputation as a humanitarian, or Einstein had been sympathetic until he became fully aware of the atrocities that the Soviet government had committed against its own citizens (how could a humanitarian be sympathetic toward a cruel regime?).

However, this did motivate me to begin an inquiry into the beliefs of Albert Einstein. It did not take long to discover that Einstein was listed by *Life* magazine (April 5, 1949) as one of the fifty "Dupes and Fellow Travelers" who were sympathetic to communist organizations. The article does not answer the question of what happened to his beliefs about the Soviet Union once he became fully aware of the Soviet atrocities, but it did prompt me to continue my search because by 1949 there was little doubt what was occurring in the Soviet Union.

The two major issues that will be presented are Einstein's ability to consistently apply standards objectively and his openness to change his viewpoint in response to new evidence. Prior to evaluating Einstein's beliefs, it is important to include some background information for appropriate context. First, Einstein had a wide range of beliefs that he liked to share with the general public (i.e., he was outspoken and did not shy away from giving opinions, even in areas in which he did not take the time to familiarize himself with, such as economics and psychology) beyond his contributions to science. Einstein, throughout his life, was especially vocal speaking out against what he believed were injustices and in support of political liberty. For example, in his book *Out of My Later Years*, Einstein (1950) made the following statement about freedom and political liberty, "I only know that I affirm them with my whole soul, and would find it intolerable to belong to a society which consistently denied them" (181). Likewise, in 1933, Einstein's (1949) views about political liberty were as follows, "As long as I have any choice, I will only stay in a country where political liberty, toleration, and equality of all citizens before the law are the rule. Political liberty implies liberty to express one's political views orally and in writing, toleration, respect for any and every individual" (81). Thus, Einstein was not only a humanitarian but possessed strong beliefs (correctly, in my view) that a repression of political freedom was intolerable.

Einstein's political views are also important for context. Specifically, Einstein was in the 1930s initially sympathetic to the Soviet government for perhaps two reasons. First, at that time, there was the looming threat of Nazism in Europe, which made many supportive of the Soviet Union, as Hitler was viewed as the larger threat (Laqueur 1990). Second, the Soviet style of government was consistent with many of Einstein's political views (e.g., he believed in a centrally planned economy). At that point, he was not alone in his beliefs, as capitalistic societies were in the midst of the depression era. Likewise, many scientists in the 1930s endorsed the Soviet system because they believed a scientific approach was necessary and had the ability to solve complex social problems (Caute 1988). Thus, to many in the intellectual and scientific communities, the Soviet Union was to become the "dictatorship of superior brains" (Caute 1988, 278) in which scientists (at least they believed at the time) would play the vital role in engineering a human society. Thus, the "masses" would be led by an intellectual elite, which was also consistent with Einstein's views of how government should operate (see Einstein 1949, 1950).

The purpose here is not to open a debate on what type of governmental system is good or bad (I understand that people can have widely divergent views on what type of political systems will be most effective) but to simply note that Einstein had an early positive belief toward the Soviet Union. As evidence to support that statement, Einstein, who was not shy about involving himself in political matters, refused to join or endorse an international commission to investigate the Moscow Show Trials, which included philosopher John Dewey. Einstein would subsequently write to Max Born that he believed the trials were legitimate (see Born 1971, 130). Born would later note that most people in the West at the time thought the trials "to be the arbitrary acts of a cruel dictator" (130). It was only those with a very sympathetic view toward the Soviet Union that did not share that interpretation. I could find no evidence (perhaps it does exist) that Einstein ever changed his belief about the fairness of the Moscow Show Trials.

The issue that is of importance, however, is Einstein's ability to accurately evaluate the Soviet Union over the years as substantial information came forth that left no doubt that the Soviet Union was a totalitarian state that did not tolerate political freedom and arbitrarily murdered and imprisoned its citizens in slave labor camps (i.e., actions wholly inconsistent with humanitarian ideals). Keep in mind that Einstein was never bashful about judging capitalism, Nazism, or other forms of government by their conduct and actions as opposed to their rhetoric, as would be expected from a humanitarian champion of freedom. However, could Einstein's positive beliefs in the Soviet style of government interfere with his ability to objectively evaluate the actions of that government? Einstein's political beliefs were very strong, but surely he would be able to objectively evaluate governmental actions, especially since he also possessed strong humanitarian ideals.

Prior to continuing this discussion of Einstein's beliefs, I believe it is important to disclose my own views about the former Soviet Union (perhaps this is simply a biased presentation of Einstein). Specifically, I believe that what Stalin did to his own people was one of the worst episodes in the history of the planet, as many were arbitrarily murdered and millions were arbitrarily put into slave labor camps (many died of starvation and cruelty in those camps). Readers are referred to Anne Applebaum's *Gulag* (2004) for a description of the Soviet concentration camps. Her chapter on what happened to women and children in the camps is especially horrific. As a point of reference, my top four most evil political leaders of the twentieth century are (1) Hitler, (2) Mao, (3) Stalin, and (4) Pol Pot. The order here is open to debate (a compelling case could be made that each deserves the top spot on the list), but all were brutal dictators who arbitrarily murdered their own citizens and did not believe in political liberty. Likewise, I view those who justify (or deny) what was done in the Soviet Union with the same disgust as those who justify (or deny) the Holocaust. How could anyone who believes in freedom, independent of specific political orientation, justify the actions of either of these murderous regimes?

So, as the accumulating evidence came forth over the years, did Einstein become a leading critic of both Stalin and the Soviet Union for their gross violations of basic human rights and political liberty that Einstein championed throughout his life? While Einstein's writings, letters, and correspondence on this issue are scattered in a wide variety of places, his communication with the philosopher Sidney Hook on this precise issue is most informative. Specifically, chapter 28, "My Running Debate with Albert Einstein," in Hook's (1987) autobiography, *Out of Step*. The chapter relies substantially upon letters exchanged between the two men (i.e., firsthand sources), and reading the chapter in its entirety will provide the reader with a greater understanding of the range of inconsistencies in Einstein's thinking when it came to his evaluation of the Soviet Union. I greatly encourage the reader to take the time to read this chapter and to read the article in the *Skeptical Inquirer* by my friend Lee Nisbet and me, which concentrates on different aspects of Einstein's inconsistencies than presented here. Furthermore, for those who are teaching courses in skepticism and critical thinking, it is interesting to have students first read Hook's chapter in a blinded format, so they are not biased by Einstein's reputation and can objectively evaluate the consistency of Einstein's reasoning.

Simply put, Einstein creates double standards for evaluating the Soviet government. He even creates a justification for the murders and slave labor camps for millions of Soviet citizens with multiple rationales (I will focus only on one here), perhaps in order to maintain the initial belief that the Soviet Union was implementing the appropriate political system. Please keep in mind that this occurred during the late 1940s and early 1950s, a time when there was no doubt about what had occurred and what was currently taking place within the Soviet Union (arbitrary murder, slave labor camps, a repression of political freedom) and when there was no longer any looming threat of Hitler and Nazism.

As one example (others exist), Einstein (1950) in his book *Out of My Later Years*, creates double standards and rationalizations for the Soviet government's brutal actions that are wholly inconsistent with his humanitarian views and belief in political liberty. Specifically, Einstein writes that "One must bear in mind that the people in Russia did not have a long political education, and changes to improve Russian conditions had to be carried through by a minority for the reason that there was no majority capable of doing it. If I had been born a Russian,

I believe I could have adjusted myself to this situation" (187). Interestingly, in the preceding paragraph, Einstein (who is advocating a world government) believes that military action should be used "to interfere in countries where a minority is oppressing a majority" (186). For the Soviet people, the majority was being oppressed, but unfortunately Einstein justified those actions. Likewise, regarding other countries in the Soviet bloc with a long "political education" that were being oppressed, like East Germany, Einstein remained silent.

Professor Hook questioned Einstein about these beliefs and rationales. Further correspondence between the two men clearly indicates that Einstein believed that in the Soviet Union it was justifiable for a select minority of individuals to subjugate the majority for "economic gains" (see Hook 1987, 476). Furthermore, Einstein even goes so far as to make the case that outsiders are in no position to criticize a murderous regime. According to Einstein (quoted in Hook 1987, 476–77), "As far as the centralization of political power and the limitation of freedom of action for the individual are concerned, I am of the opinion that these restrictions should not exceed the limit demanded by exterior security, inner stability, and the necessities resulting from a planned economy. An outsider is hardly able to judge the facts and possibilities." Einstein was never, as an outsider, shy about judging the facts when it came to political repression in other countries and has been appropriately commended for his willingness to speak out against such actions. As previously mentioned, he was recommending military action in other cases. Sadly, Einstein also seems more concerned about the Soviet government's meddling in "intellectual and artistic matters" (quoted in Hook 1987, 476) than about the fate of the average citizen living in terror.

Even Einstein's good friend, Max Born (1971), found Einstein's views toward political liberty and the Soviet Union "hard to reconcile" (131) with his humanitarian character. Unfortunately, Einstein was not alone, as numerous intellectuals, perhaps captivated by the lofty goals of communism, refused to either believe the shocking actions of the Soviet government or created a variety of justifications for a murderous and brutal regime (Caute 1988; Hook 1987; Sowell 1996).

Interestingly, Anne Applebaum (2004), in her introduction to *Gulag*, discusses the inconsistent reactions of people to equally horrific governmental actions. In one anecdotal observation, she viewed the actions in the newly freed Prague, where one could purchase Soviet bits and pieces such as pins and hats. She notes (xviii), "Most of the people buying the Soviet paraphernalia were Americans and West Europeans. All would be sickened by the thought of wearing a swastika. None objected, however, to wearing the hammer and sickle on a T-shirt or a hat. It was a minor observation, but sometimes, it is through just such minor observations that a cultural mood is best observed. For here the lesson could not have been clearer: while the symbol of one mass murder fills us with horror, the symbol of another mass murder makes us laugh."

At this point, it is also important to evaluate the claim that mass murders and slave labor camps in the Soviet Union actually achieved economic and social benefits that could not otherwise have occurred, which is the crux of Einstein's rationale to justify what had taken place. As Einstein notes (cited in Hook 1987, 477), "[I]t cannot be doubted that the achievements of the Soviet regime are considerable in the fields of education, public health, social welfare, and economics, and that the people as a whole have greatly gained by these achievements." This statement provides evidence that Einstein abandoned his critical thinking skills, because as a scientist he must have known that the gains have to be compared against a control condition to exclude the possibility (or great likelihood here) that they could not have been achieved in other ways. Specifically, the notion that conditions involving workers who are murdered, severely malnourished, terrorized, tortured, beaten, raped, arbitrarily separated from family and friends, exposed to harsh weather without proper clothing, placed in jobs in which they do not possess the proper training and skills, and so on was the only way to make positive economic achievements is nonsense. Einstein must have either uncritically accepted Soviet propaganda about the achievements of the gulags and/or never considered the possibility that humane treatment of citizens could have accomplished (or exceeded) the same objectives.

This type of rationale creating and abandoning of critical thinking is still repeated today in some intellectual circles, perhaps as a way to maintain political beliefs (e.g., Stalin really wasn't that bad, look at all the good he accomplished that would have otherwise not occurred). However, the Soviet archives (i.e., the historical record) that documented worker productivity tell a vastly different story. Once again, while Soviet propaganda highlighted the contributions of the slave labor camps (the sheer size of the camps made some contributions possible), the Soviet records contradict the propaganda. As Applebaum (2004, 109) notes, "Prison labor had always been—and would always be—far less productive than free labor." Likewise, as economist Thomas Sowell (2004, 54) notes, "But just the purely economic costs—quite aside from the staggering human costs—were typically higher than the cost of doing the same things outside the gulags. For example, the cost of producing bricks in a facility with forced labor was more than double the cost of producing them in a nearby Soviet brick factory." Keep in mind that the Soviet economy as a whole was not very productive, so in comparison the gulags were extremely inefficient from a solely economic perspective, and the costs of the guards alone exacerbated the problem (Applebaum 2004). As Sowell (2004, 53) points out, "[T]he forced labor of the inmates still did not cover the costs of the gulags. Shortly after Stalin's death, the head of the Soviet secret police—hardly a humanitarian—began closing the camps down for economic reasons." Thus, the still-repeated myth today, that the gulags and Stalin's methods were necessary as the only way to make progress for the Soviet people, is not supported by historical facts. In fact, the Soviet archives document that the Soviet people were worse off economically because of the gulags, not better.

In summary, Einstein provides an example that even a brilliant mind is not immune from the cognitive and emotional biases that have evolved in the human species to strengthen and maintain beliefs once formed. Despite the fact that he was a humanitarian and cherished political liberty for the individual citizen throughout his life, he ultimately discarded his own beliefs for the Soviet people, ignored widespread evidence, created double standards for evaluation, and even created justifications for the murders and slave labor camps of millions of Soviet citizens in order to maintain his positive views toward the Soviet style of government. Einstein had no problem evaluating other types of governments by their actions (and should be commended for that), but he judged the Soviet Union based upon its hopes and dreams while discounting its actions. For the ambitious student, it may be an interesting project to compare and contrast Einstein's views and rationalizations toward the Soviet Union with Sir Arthur Conan Doyle's views and rationalizations toward the supernatural. I believe you will find that both men did not use their critical thinking skills and were ultimately influenced by their preexisting beliefs.

Part III

EXAMPLES OF
INCONSISTENT CRITICAL THINKING

The Influence of Our Beliefs

In contrast with parts I and II, whose purpose was to introduce the reader to some of the hallmarks of critical thinking and discuss an evolutionary framework of why and how our beliefs influence our individual critical thinking, respectively, part III will use a variety of differing claims and issues to point out potential examples of inconsistent critical thinking. These examples were selected primarily because I believe (the reader is certainly free to disagree) that a critical inquiry raises concerns or provides evidence in contrast to the prevailing opinions of many critical thinkers on these topics. For example, the first issue to be addressed is global warming, a contemporary issue about which many individuals have very strong beliefs. The intent here is not to solve the problem or provide the reader with "the truth" on this issue—that is well beyond the expertise of the author, and I believe currently no concrete answer exists yet on this topic. The purpose is to use the issue to determine if consistent standards of critical thinking are being applied. One of the most disappointing aspects about the current global warming debate is just how many people, on both sides of the issue, have strong opinions on a topic they have not even taken the time to subject to a rudimentary skeptical inquiry.

Likewise, repeated political and multicultural claims will be used in a similar fashion, to illustrate how inconsistently critical thinking is often applied to various claims. I will attempt to directly compare economists with skeptics, as both groups have made similar arguments and complaints over the years. Although I am not an economist, I have attempted to familiarize myself over the years with the basics of the discipline, as our fields (economics and psychology) often cross over and cover similar topics (e.g., the influence of the perception of physical attractiveness on various outcome variables; see Riniolo, Johnson, Sherman, and Misso 2006), and there exists overlap between the assumptions that economics and psychology make when interpreting data and events. Thus, I hope I am not deviating too far from my own area of competence and will do justice to economists in this chapter. In fact, I can think of no subject area on which more individuals have strong opinions than economics yet do not apply their normal critical thinking skills, which is why this chapter is included in this book.

Finally, I hope the reader will be kind enough to indulge me in the final chapter of part III. Perhaps this chapter is too personal and should not be included. However, I dislike when Santa Claus is attacked with baseless claims that good old St. Nick undermines critical thinking later in life. Thus, I will try to point out why these attacks are not grounded in any compelling evidence and are in contrast to contemporary theory about what determines normal cognitive development.

Chapter 10

GLOBAL WARMING AND PSYCHIC CLAIMS

A Comparison

To scientists, these seemingly disparate incidents represent the advance signs of fundamental changes in the world's weather. The central fact is that after three quarters of a century of extraordinarily mild conditions, the earth's climate seems to be cooling down.
— *Newsweek*, "The Cooling World" (April 28, 1975, p. 64)

Let's start this chapter with a pop quiz. First question: Is global warming occurring? Second question: What is responsible for global warming if it is occurring? Third question: What are the consequences for us if global warming is occurring? Based upon my reading of skeptical publications, I'm assuming that many readers believe the earth is warming substantially, that human activity (e.g., CO_2 emissions) is largely responsible for global warming, and that some dire consequences are likely to occur (e.g., rising sea temperatures, increases in violent weather) if something is not done to counteract the current trend. The focus of this chapter is not actually on global warming (although that topic will be discussed) but on using global warming to illustrate potential inconsistent critical thinking.

I would like to ask a final question, aimed particularly at those readers with strong opinions on the topic of global warming: Where does your information about global warming come from? Be honest. If the answer to the question is primarily or exclusively media reports (e.g., the nightly news, newspaper reports, television specials, magazines), then an adequate critical evaluation on this topic has not been carried out. At the heart of critical thinking is the evidence-demanding attitude, and being solely or primarily influenced by media reports is a passive way of evaluating a claim, especially since firsthand materials (e.g., surface temperature readings, satellite readings, journal articles) are widely available and can be obtained with minimal effort.

Keep in mind, this is the same media that we routinely chastise for perpetuating such myths as King Tut's curse, the Bermuda Triangle, and repressed memories, to name just a few. As one example, the *New York Times* (the "paper of record") was responsible for helping to legitimize the notion that the house in Amityville, New York, was haunted (see Kaplan and Kaplan 1995). As Nickell (2003, 13) points out, "Although the original event proved to be a hoax, that fact does not seem well known to the general public." In addition, ABC's *Primetime Thursday* (October 31, 2002) presented the story as likely genuine on Halloween (see Christopher 2003). Nobody within the skeptical community was surprised, as the "haunted" version is a much better story. Most critical thinkers believe the media is biased with a pro-paranormal slant. If the media can so easily dismiss facts when presenting issues related to the paranormal, everyone should wonder what other factual information is dismissed when reporting. Simply put, one of the standards for critical thinking is not to rely solely upon media reporting for important information even if that media reporting is eventually corroborated by your independent critical evaluation (the media does report that exercise is good for you). Critical thinking is an active, not passive, method to gather and evaluate information, and one of the hallmarks of critical thinking is to be skeptical of secondhand information (e.g., see chapter 4).

So, is the media reporting on global warming accurate? Please note that for every inaccurate media account about the paranormal over the past fifteen years, a similar amount of inaccurate reporting has occurred about issues related to the environment and global warming. As just one of many examples, the *New York Times* (August 19, 2000) reported on the *front page* that "The North Pole Is Melting" and that the last time this occurred was some fifty million years ago (the implication was that global warming was the likely culprit). To make a rather long story short (readers are referred to Michaels 2004, *Meltdown*, for a more detailed presentation of this story and many other examples of media outlets misrepresenting issues related to global warming), the *Times* retreated from this story by August 29. Minimal fact checking (this was a page one story!) would have shown that the ice conditions in the late summer were not out of the ordinary and that similar conditions have occurred many times within the past fifty million years. Michaels (2004, 42) describes the reporting as "a wonderful example of scientific doomsaying that ignores a few inconvenient facts."

Unfortunately, there have been a wide range of stories that not only ignore facts on issues related to global warming but link or blame global warming for every type of normal weather event (e.g., El Niño, hurricanes, tornados, summer heat waves, floods, and even snowstorms) without scientific evidence for the connection (see Cerveny 2005 for a review). This type of "doomsaying" reporting does nothing more than interfere with our ability to make accurate assessments of what actually is happening and may serve to increase the chances of individuals accepting such weak evidence as isolated personal experiences (e.g., a warm week in the winter) as compelling evidence of climate change. In contrast, others may dismiss all positive evidence of climate change out of hand as just another example of media hype. Yet, like the reporting on the house in Amityville, this type of "journalism" does make for a more interesting story.

If the media were actually interested in informing the public, the general public would know that most of the recorded warming in the Northern Hemisphere after World War II (a) occurs during the winter months (approximately 69 percent) and (b) is disproportionately occurring in the coldest portions of the world (see Balling, Michaels, and Knappenberger 1998; Michaels and Balling 2000; Michaels, Knappenberger, Balling, and Davis 2000). This is exactly what is predicted by the greenhouse theory because the warming from carbon dioxide is influenced by water vapor (very dry air, most often found in winter, warms the most). Specifically, Michaels et al. (2000) demonstrated that the winter warming is largely confined (approximately 78 percent) to the extremely cold and dry high-pressure systems of northwestern North America and Siberia, which is a relatively small area (26 percent). Thus, warming is not uniformly global but largely isolated and unevenly distributed throughout the year. However, a media report of "Siberia Warming in Winter, But Still Frozen Solid" is not as catchy as "The North Pole Is Melting." At least the former is supported by evidence, whereas the latter will likely sell more newspapers.

With that information in mind, the purpose of this chapter is not to settle the global warming debate. That issue is beyond the expertise of the author and cannot at this point be settled even by the experts in the area (only time, more accurate measurements, and more data will provide some answers). However, as an advocate of critical thinking, I would hope that we can all agree that prior to simply accepting that practically meaningful global warming is occurring (especially the apocalyptic predictions) and is being strongly influenced by human activity (the two could largely be independent of each other), or simply dismissing the claim out of hand, we should consistently apply critical thinking to this important claim (i.e., ask critical questions, read firsthand reports, rigorously evaluate experimental methods, question secondhand sources). Of course, the significant question about human activity is not if we contribute to climate change (taken to a logical extreme, this seems obvious) but how much human activity does contribute and the implications of that activity (which could range from virtually nothing to extremely important; there are disagreements about these issues). I must admit, the current winter warming in Siberia does not worry me at the moment, especially since the greatest amount of global warming occurs at night, when temperatures are coldest (Easterling et al. 1997).

It should be noted that the majority of scientists who investigate climate and climate change do believe that global warming is occurring (although the consensus is not of the doomsday variety, which is often given greater media attention) and that human activity is contributing. Does that mean that we should simply defer to the experts, as they do possess some advantages over the novice (see chapter 2) and not actively seek out information and perform our own investigation? According to Carl Sagan (1996), in the now classic *Demon-Haunted World*, the answer is clearly no! My Baloney Detection Kit, obtained from the Skeptics Society (see www.skeptics.com), also says no! Leading skeptic Michael Shermer (2001), in *Why People Believe Weird Things*, also says no! As philosopher Sidney Hook (2002, 99) notes, "The fact is that experts are sometimes wrong. This does not prove that amateurs are as good or better than experts but only that experts are not infallible and therefore, where our own welfare is at stake, we must do our own thinking." Finally, we should also not simply defer to the experts because the history of science continually reminds us that the prevailing opinion of today is often the laughingstock of tomorrow, so applying critical thinking to any claim, especially one of such potential importance, is warranted.

Thus, as a skeptic with no specific expertise in climatology (although I do possess research and statistical expertise; for example, see Riniolo 1997, 1999; Riniolo and Porges 1997, 2000; Riniolo and Schmidt 2000), I will first present some issues that arose in my critical inquiry into the global warming issue (yes, I actually looked at the data!). After this presentation (it is not meant to be exhaustive or to change any minds on the issue), the remainder of the chapter will place side by side the standards that skeptics have traditionally used to evaluate psychic claims with the current claims for global warming. Once again, the purpose of this chapter is to highlight potential inconsistent critical thinking.

A NONEXPERT'S SKEPTICAL INQUIRY

First, the earth's surface temperature has changed throughout history, typically within a relatively narrow band. Thus, temperature change

Figure 10.1

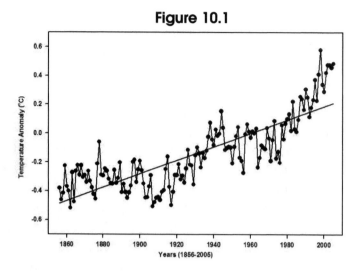

is normal, and recent changes may or may not be part of a normal process. The causes of the change historically are not particularly clear, but the recent changes are believed by most scientists to be influenced by human activity. Attempts to quantify the annual global temperatures began in the 1850s, when a global network of thermometer readings was created that uses both sea and land readings. Fortunately, everyone has access to this data, which can be obtained from several sources, such as NASA. This chapter has relied upon data obtained from the Climatic Research Unit in England (http://www.cru.uea.ac.uk/; see specifically http://www.cru.uea.ac.uk/ftpdata/tavegl2v.dat), which is a widely used database for climate researchers. Figure 10.1 shows the overall upward trend from 1856 to 2005 (the anomaly values are from the base period 1961 to 1990).

Looking at the data for the twentieth century (problems with accurately quantifying surface temperatures will be addressed later), three interesting patterns emerge. First, the early portion of the century (1901–1940; see figure 10.2) was characterized by warming, the next forty years (1941–1980; see figure 10.3) was characterized by no change in temperature (portions of this forty-year period led most scientists at the time to conclude that the earth was heading into a long-

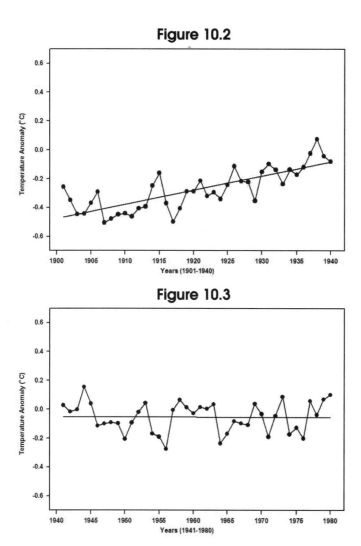

Figure 10.2

Figure 10.3

term cooling pattern), and the last twenty years show another warming trend (1981–2000; see figure 10.4). Human activity resulted in progressively more CO_2 being released into the atmosphere throughout the century. This data illustrates that CO_2 levels from human activity are not the only factor that influences surface temperature and, more importantly, that patterns can shift over relatively long periods of time (i.e., forty years or so).

Figure 10.4

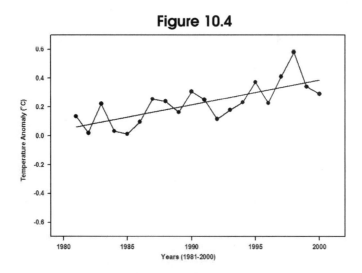

In addition, if the temperature pattern of the twentieth century is broken into five twenty-year segments, the following pattern emerges: 1901–1920 (a statistically nonsignificant trend toward warming); 1921–1940 (a statistically significant warming); 1941–1960 (a statistically nonsignificant trend toward cooling); 1961–1980 (a statistically nonsignificant trend toward warming); 1981–2000 (a statistically significant warming). Interestingly, of the two statistically significant periods (see figure 10.5), the warming was slightly greater from 1921 to 1940 compared with 1981 to 2000 (once again, CO_2 levels were lower in this earlier time segment).

If the temperature pattern of the twentieth century is broken into quarters, the following emerges: 1901–1925 (a statistically nonsignificant trend toward warming); 1926–1950 (a statistically significant warming); 1951–1975 (a statistically nonsignificant trend toward cooling); 1976–2000 (a statistically significant warming). Here, the last quarter of the century had the greatest warming, although just slightly greater than the 1921–1940 segment.

I hope that presenting the data in this fashion illustrates several points. First, a variety of trends occurred in the twentieth century, and the trends do not always link with rising CO_2 levels. Second, based

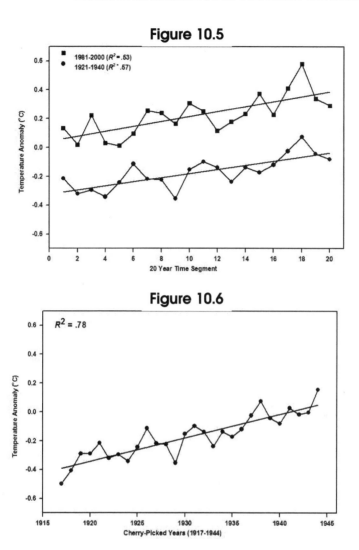

Figure 10.5

Figure 10.6

upon where the time segment is started and ended, differing numbers can occur. I resisted (although many "global warming" advocates do not) "cherry-picking" segments that could have made the numbers look even more compelling or suspicious depending on how I chose to present the data. Starting or ending a time segment with high or low scores is the easiest way to accomplish this goal. See figure 10.6 for an example from 1917 to 1944, which shows a very strong warming trend. In fact, this warming trend is much stronger than the warming at the end of the twentieth century and was followed by a long period (about thirty-five years) of no temperature change.

Simply put, trends longer than twenty to twenty-five years are needed to accurately assess the data. Note that the current predictions of warming did not occur until the late 1980s/early 1990s. Thus, the current segment of data is less than twenty years old, since the a priori prediction that warming would occur (working backward to include the 1980s is cherry-picking, especially since cooling was predicted to occur in the 1980s). The clock starts once the prediction is made (this is the standard that we as critical thinkers would use for an evaluation of a psychic). There is less than twenty years of data for this a priori prediction that warming is occurring. Given that changes have appeared after the warming that occurred in the early portion of the century (about forty years worth of data), asking for more data is warranted.

(A quick side note. For readers who looked at figure 10.4, and were wondering what the warming "spike" was in the late 1990s, the answer is that was the 1998 El Niño, which is widely believed to be responsible for the increased temperature and is not the result of global warming. Note that 1998 is a good year to start a time series and predict cooling because outlier data can influence trends much more at the beginning or end of a time series, which is well known by those who cherry-pick time segments to exaggerate claims. At the time of this writing, no year after 1998 has been higher in terms of warming. You can check into the future by visiting the Climatic Research Unit Web site (http://www.cru.uea.ac.uk/).

If I were the devious attention-seeking type, I could, on January 1, 1999, have called a press conference and claimed that by psychic powers I would keep the earth from further warming. With some scientists claiming that global warming was going to rapidly accelerate and that the planet was heading for disaster—combined with the media's love of a good psychic and global warming story—I'm sure I could now be known as the psychic who single-handedly stopped global warming in its tracks for x number of years. Stay tuned, you may see me after the next El Niño year!)

The current theory regarding global warming is an example of what is known as an "ex post facto study." Ex post facto studies observe a current outcome (e.g., a trend toward warming) and attempt to look back in time to find the causal variable (e.g., at this time, the most plausible is human influence, but others exist). Unfortunately, this type of research design does not allow researchers to manipulate variables and implement controls for rival hypotheses (the same criticism is made when a Freudian therapist attempts to find a cause of a known outcome by searching the patient's past, as no controls for alternative explanations are used). As one example, to my knowledge, the influence of greenhouse gases released into the atmosphere by termites and other insects, which is substantial (Zimmerman, Greenberg, Wandiga, and Crutzen 1982), has not been adequately controlled. Campbell and Stanley (1966, 64), in their now classic book on research design, have correctly noted that ex post facto experiments are "unsatisfactory at their very best." Michael Shermer (2001, 53) notes that this type of after-the-fact reasoning is at its basest level "a form of superstition."

An after-the-fact type of research design should be viewed with caution because it cannot rule out other plausible alternative hypotheses (e.g., is the patient depressed because of an unresolved sexual conflict or does a more parsimonious explanation exist, such as a recent loss of a loved one?). Ex post facto designs are very useful to generate testable hypotheses for the future (that's what Darwin's theory did), but at this point, there is simply not enough data to have great confidence in predictions for long-term trends. I have limited confidence in less than twenty years' worth of data (let's say 1990 is the starting point), because shifts in temperature in the twentieth century occurred after forty years, and such shifts can potentially occur after even longer periods of time.

As a specific example of why ex post facto research should be treated with great caution, it is important to keep in mind that the a priori prediction from many scientists in the mid- to late 1970s was that the earth was going to cool (see opening quote of this chapter), not heat up. It's much easier to find a posteriori reasons why something occurs than to predict the future, as many psychics have found out. These predictions of cooling certainly seemed just as compelling at the time as the current predictions of warming, especially since at the end of the 1970s the United States experienced the three worst consecutive winters in the modern weather record (Michaels 2004; in Buffalo, we had the Blizzard of '77). Some scientists even recommended that portions of the polar ice caps should be melted to counteract the "impending" ice age (fortunately, that did not occur) and were making forecasts of catastrophic famines resulting from the predicted climate change. With such recent predictions being spectacularly wrong (arrived at from ex post facto information), should we as critical thinkers accept future predictions at face value or should we wait until a proven track record of predictions occurs? The standard for evaluating a psychic is a proven track record. Economist Julian Simon (1995, 646) nicely summarizes this issue:

> Remember that only a decade or so before the global warming scare got going—in the middle 1970s—the very persons and institutions that now scold us about taking action to reduce global warming were raising the alarm about global cooling. That is, it took only about a decade for the switch from one scenario of doom to the opposite. The worriers about cooling included *Science*, the most influential scientific journal in the world, quoting an official of the World Meteorological Organization; the National Academy of Sciences worrying about the onset of a 10,000 year ice age; *Newsweek*, warning that food production could be adversely affected within a decade; the *New York Times* quoting an official of the National Center for Atmospheric Research; and *Science Digest* . . .

With that information in mind, let me clearly state that I do not know with certainty if warming is occurring, nor do I know if human activities are significantly contributing to the warming if it is occurring. My current opinion on this topic, after my critical inquiry into this issue (which will be elaborated on below), is that (a) the preponderance of the evidence (still not beyond a reasonable doubt) is consistent with a recent modest warming that will not lead to the doomsday scenarios that are often hyped in the media, (b) the influ-ence of human behavior on this modest warming is still unclear, (c) there still exists methodological issues in data collection and analysis that need further clarification to more precisely measure global tem-peratures, and (d) the scientific literature on this topic provides a much more fuzzy picture than the sound bites that are disseminated in secondhand sources. Certainly other critical thinkers can arrive at a different conclusion than my interpretation because of the ambi-guity of some of the results on this issue. However, there is a vast dif-ference between individuals who have performed their own skeptical inquiry and arrived at different conclusions and those whose opinions at this point are primarily the result of media reports.

Once again, I am not an expert in this field, which does put me at a disadvantage when evaluating some of the specific claims being made in this debate. However, the important issue for this chapter is the consistency of applying the methods of critical thinking to impor-tant claims. For example, how could a critical thinker have a strong belief on this issue either way (dismissing the claims out of hand is equally troubling because of the potential important implications) without actually looking at the data? Likewise, I do believe that dif-ferent standards of evidence are being applied to the acceptance of the theory of global warming and humans' contribution to global warming by some critical thinkers, especially those who classify this issue as a proven "fact." The most likely reason perhaps is critical thinkers' willingness as a group to place great faith in the scientific community (which is typically justified, as critical thinking requires scientific evidence when evaluating claims), combined here with an overall message that is positive and easy to support (i.e., who doesn't want a cleaner environment?). Of course, there are serious economic implications that need to be considered when evaluating the proposed remedies for global warming that are beyond the scope of this chapter but that should be part of the overall debate.

Who could possibly need to seek out discrediting evidence for a scientific claim that is linked to a cleaner environment? Well, critical thinkers do, as nothing is off-limits! In order to illustrate exactly how the traditional skeptical standards are being inconsistently applied to the global warming debate, I thought it would be interesting to seek out discrediting evidence, place side by side the same standards skeptics have traditionally applied to psychic claims, and then apply those same standards to the theory of global warming.

SKEPTICAL STANDARDS APPLIED TO
CLAIMS OF GLOBAL WARMING

Methodological Problems

The history of parapsychology is fraught with methodological problems. Thus, parapsychological research cannot exclude more parsimonious explanations that "psychic powers" exist (readers are referred to *A Skeptic's Handbook of Parapsychology*, Kurtz 1985, for some of the more interesting historical examples). For example, outright fraud, inappropriate safeguards to prevent potential cheating, and simple methodological problems (e.g., insufficient randomization) have all occurred. Likewise, skeptics, in seeking discrediting evidence, have gone through the procedures with a fine-tooth comb looking for methodological problems with experiments. For example, the Pearce-Pratt experiment (Hubert Pearce obtained high scores guessing ESP cards in two conditions) had previously been presented by parapsychologists as scientific evidence of paranormal abilities. Dr. Hansel, skeptical of the results, visited Dr. Pratt and had him re-create the testing procedures. After a "critical analysis" of the experiment, Dr. Hansel (1961, 91) concluded that "the experimental conditions were such that above-chance scores could have been obtained by means of a trick, this experiment cannot be cited as providing evidence for ESP."

As a more recent example, psychologist Daryl Bem and parapsychologist Charles Honorton (1994) presented evidence of telepathy using the ganzfeld procedure, which seeks to minimize distractions using sensory deprivation techniques. Skeptics have questioned (and rightly so) the results of these experiments because of procedural details that may have introduced a bias responsible for the results (see Hyman 1994; Milton and Wiseman 1999). The experimental details were rigorously evaluated in an attempt to identify methodological uncertainties.

When methodological problems occur in testing psychics, the more parsimonious answer (see chapter 3) is to simply say that until the methodological problems are corrected, we cannot conclude that measurement error or uncontrolled variables are not responsible for the results. Thus, in testing a psychic when measurement error is present, we cannot exclude the simpler possibility that sensory information (not psychic powers) was somehow uncontrolled and responsible for the results. For example, in the case of the Pearce-Pratt experiment, opportunity for cheating by the subject occurred and is at this point the more parsimonious explanation. Thus, the standard for testing a psychic is that methodological problems are not acceptable.

Like the studies investigating psychic occurrences, there have been problems with measurement error in attempting to accurately quantify global temperatures. The reader should not be under the misconception—for any of the data sets used by climatologists investigating global climate change—that measuring global temperatures is a simple task that gives completely objective data independent of human judgments. Specifically, because of biases in all the data sets, "[a]djustments are complicated, sometimes as large as the trend itself, involve expert judgments, and cannot be stringently evaluated because of lack of traceable standards" (Christy et al. 2006, 29). Thus, the reader should think of the temperature readings as "estimates" as opposed to "exact" representations of global temperatures.

As a specific example with the surface readings (many others exist, see Balling 2005; Christy et al. 2006; Mears et al. 2006), there is a problem known as the "urban heat island" or "urban bias," which causes a bias when investigating global surface temperatures. This is a source of measurement error (it appears that the urban heat island has been underestimated) that influences long-term climate records as cities have grown up around some measurement sites. This bias does not appear to be as easily "removed" as researchers had earlier believed (see McKendry 2003 for a discussion of this issue). I was surprised to learn exactly how this bias was typically handled by climatologists. Specifically, urban bias (a complex phenomenon with multiple feedback loops) was typically "controlled" by using population size as the indicator of the bias with a simple regression (imagine controlling just one variable as an indicator of any complex phenomena, which likely explains why removing the bias accurately is more complicated than previously thought). Furthermore, using regression in this way to control a variable is potentially problematic because if the assumptions of the statistical test are not met, the results can be misleading.

In addition, the problems with removing the urban bias are not the only sources of potential error. As Michaels and Balling (2000, 79) note, "What is more, these thermometric surface air temperature estimates are fraught with other problems as well, including the lack of data in remote and oceanic areas, changes in the network over the past century, changes in instruments and observation practices, and microclimatic changes near the weather equipment, such as a growing tree near a weather station."

Likewise, research has also indicated that land-use changes due to agriculture also cause positively biased readings (Kalnay and Cai 2003). Interestingly, when the corrections to control for changes in land use when investigating the average temperature in the United States include the influence of agriculture, there was no trend toward warming in the twentieth century (Michaels 2005). Furthermore, the sea temperature readings have their own problems (Christy et al. 2006), and "all known bias adjustments have not yet been applied to sea surface temperature data" (Mears et al. 2006, 71). What is of importance, and what is unknown at this point, is the cumulative influence of all the potential sources of measurement bias, how the bias is distributed, are the current methods to remove the bias adequate, and is the remaining bias comparable to the actual climate change that has been identified, which is small? Thus, measurement error with surface temperature readings has not yet been sufficiently ruled out as an important influence on global temperature estimates.

So, how can researchers minimize the potential bias associated with the surface temperature readings? Fortunately, satellite temperature readings of the troposphere (the zone five thousand to thirty thousand feet above the earth's surface) are available. The troposphere minimizes problems associated with the earth's surface and can provide data that is truly global (as opposed to the limited surface network). In addition, greenhouse theory predicts more warming here than at the surface. Unfortunately, unlike the surface temperatures, which date back to the 1850s, the satellite readings provide a much smaller time series. Specifically, the Microwave Sounding Unit (MSU) provides data starting in December 1978 (see Spencer and Christy 1990).

The satellite temperature readings (sounds like there should be no measurement issues here with such highly technical equipment) also have measurement bias (e.g., orbit decay, orbit drift) that must be corrected (Christy, Spencer, and Braswell 2000; Lanzante et al. 2006; Mears et al. 2006). Furthermore, it is unknown if other biases remain in the satellite data, but given that biases have been so recently identified, it is not prudent to assume that none now exist.

To add to the complexity of the discussion, which is often oversimplified in secondhand sources or sound bite summaries of scientific papers, it should be pointed out that there currently exist three research groups—University of Alabama in Huntsville, Remote Sensing Systems, and University of Maryland—that analyze data (from various portions of the troposphere) from the MSU satellite data sets. All three groups have to correct for drifts in diurnal sampling, which creates a bias in the data, and different methods exist to merge data from the multiple satellites (see Mears et al. 2006 for further elaboration). Thus, subjective decisions (each with strengths and weaknesses; Lanzante et al. 2006) that differ between all three groups exist in analyzing the same satellite data. Remember that scientists have a long history of being influenced by expectation (see chapter 3), which further complicates matters, as no data set exists that is free of human decision making.

For example, all three groups show recent warming but all differ on the important question of how much, as meaningful differences exist between the warming estimates calculated by the three groups (see Lanzante et al. 2006, 61, table 3.3). As Mears et al. (2006, 80) note, "These differences are an excellent example of structural uncertainty, where identical input data and three seemingly reasonable methodologies lead to trends that differ significantly more than the amount expected given their reported internal uncertainties." It is unknown at this point which group is most closely approximating the true temperature change.

Likewise, should we arbitrarily pick one group's estimates of global temperatures over the other two? I agree with Mears et al. (2006, 87), "We could make value-based judgments to imply increased confidence in certain data sets, but these would not be unambiguous, may eventually be proven wrong, and are not a tenable approach in the longer term from a scientific perspective. Therefore, tools need to be developed to objectively discriminate between data sets." For the interested reader, the most recent report issued by the US Climate Change Science Program (April 2006; *Temperature Trends in the Lower Atmosphere: Steps for Understanding and Reconciling Differences*) addresses a wide variety of issues related to quantification of global temperatures from various data sets (e.g., surface readings, weather balloons, satellites; this report is available at http://www.climate science.gov/Library/sap/sap1-1/finalreport/default.htm). What is salient about the report is just how much has been learned about measurement error in the last ten years, and how much yet remains in need of further clarification. Once again, no reader should be under the misconception that accurately measuring global temperatures is a simple task, free of measurement error, and independent of human judgment. (I personally wish more energy was focused toward accurate quantification of global temperatures at this point, as opposed to attempting to make future predictions about global climate change.)

It would be interesting to learn exactly how specific findings are chosen to be emphasized and ultimately disseminated to the media and general public by governmental agencies that are influential for public policy decisions. For example, the Intergovernmental Panel on Climate Change (IPCC) was established by the United Nations and

conducts assessments of climate change and climate forecasts. However, the reports issued by the IPCC do not go through the regular
peer review process, and the groups themselves are strongly influenced by bureaucrats as well as scientists. As a specific example of
selective presentation (perhaps the confirmation bias at work) that
oversimplifies the whole picture, the IPCC in its 1996 *Assessment* left
out data that were at that time inconsistent with a warming trend (the
report only highlighted data consistent with warming; Michaels
2004). Thus, readers such as journalists and policy makers were given
a misleading impression about the certainty of the overall data. Perhaps another "Project Alpha" (see chapter 2) would be necessary to
get a true understanding of just what actually does occur when subjective decisions about which data to "highlight" are made in these
types of institutions.

In summary, the critical thinker does not accept results with
methodological problems as conclusive in a psychic investigation. At
this point, methodological issues and potential problems with data
collection and analysis have not been ruled out or sufficiently
resolved. Once again, while I believe the preponderance of the evidence indicates a modest recent warming, the methodological uncertainty that exists does not allow me to say that warming is a "fact" and
that it will automatically continue in the future. I do believe (just an
outsider's opinion here, so take it for what it's worth) that the satellite
readings eventually can go a long way in providing the necessary data
to accurately estimate how much and in what areas the earth is
warming, remaining constant, or cooling. However, in order to accurately accomplish that goal, a larger time series is needed (i.e., many
more years of data collection), and improvements must occur in the
quantification and analysis of the data to ensure that biases have been
adequately removed. Likewise, the notion that only three groups (no
disrespect to any of the groups, as they should be commended for
taking on this important task) are analyzing the satellite data is somewhat troubling because of the subjective decision making that must be
made to process and analyze the data. Moreover, additional groups
would likely increase the chances of identifying additional biases that

are potentially undetected at this point. Thus, I would love to see more groups become involved in analyzing the satellite data (i.e., the more "brains" working on this issue, the better).

THE STANDARD OF CONSISTENCY

Psychics are well known in the skeptical literature for their failed predictions. In fact, Gene Emery has been tracking the success of psychic predictions since the late 1970s, and his evaluations often appear in *Skeptical Inquirer*. To say the least, the predictions do not have a very successful track record, for example, Madonna did not marry Boy George. And, of course, nobody predicted the tragedy of 9/11 or the death of Princess Diana.

However, every now and again, some strange event does occur (e.g., a psychic prediction comes true; the patient of a psychic healer recovers from a serious illness; a dream predicting some future event occurs). How do critical thinkers explain these types of events, which are presented by psychics as real evidence of supernatural occurrences? If you remember from chapter 4, coincidences (i.e., odd or "supernatural" occurrences) are normal in the larger context of probabilities. Thus, in order to get a better understanding of how "strange" some event actually is, the event itself must be placed in the context of all possible events (e.g., an individual purchasing a ticket and winning the lottery is a strange event; any individual winning the lottery, from the millions of tickets purchased, is a normal event given the mathematical odds). For example, the case of a patient of a psychic healer who recovers from a serious illness has no meaning on its own unless we know how many patients the psychic has treated (some patients will spontaneously improve with no treatment or with a placebo treatment). Thus, if the psychic has treated thousands of patients and one recovers, that is very different than if the psychic is able to consistently heal many people. Simply put, the standard for the critical thinker in evaluating a psychic claim is not to accept an isolated finding but to insist upon a demonstration of consistent results (i.e., psychic investigations must be replicated to establish the consistency of results).

Does the evidence for global warming meet the standard of consistency? Anyone interested in this issue has likely seen on television (once again, media reporting is an example of a secondhand source and should not be accepted at face value) huge icebergs breaking off from the Antarctic Peninsula (an isolated event). However, the sea ice has increased, and the Antarctic surface has shown a small cooling trend recently (i.e., inconsistent findings; see Comiso 2000; Doran et al. 2002; Parkinson 2002, Thompson and Solomon 2002; Vyas et al. 2003). Also, in west Antarctica, there has been ice-sheet growth of the Ross Ice Streams (Joughin and Tulaczyk 2002).

The number of icebergs worldwide is substantial, approximately 160,000. If the whole context is examined, rather than a few isolated events, there are inconsistent findings. As Braithwaite (2002, 92) notes, "There is no obvious common global trend of increasing glacier melt in recent years, and the data mainly reflect variations on intra- and inter-regional scales, which need more study in future." A recent study (Johannessen, Khvorostovsky, Miles, Bobylev 2005) indicates that the ice sheet in the interior of Greenland above 1,500 meters has increased from 1992, while there has been a decrease below 1,500 meters. Also, differing trends have been detected in the Northern Hemisphere compared with the Southern Hemisphere (Michaels and Balling 2000). Other examples exist, but the main point is that results are inconsistent when one looks at the global trends (i.e., warming here, but cooling or no change there).

Martin Gardner, an expert on the issue of the problems of interpreting potentially isolated events, summarizes this issue nicely. Once again, the issue for this chapter is applying standards consistently to both paranormal and environmental claims. As Gardner points out (1998, 15–16):

> A parapsychologist reports an unusual number of hits (or misses) in a run of 100 trials. ESP or clumping? It is impossible to tell without knowing how many tests were made, not only by that parapsychologist but also by others around the world. If a thousand scientists, in

different parts of the world, toss a hundred pennies in the air, some of the outcomes will show an astonishing number of heads. If only these tests are reported, and we have no knowledge of the others, it will be impossible to make an accurate evaluation of the reported tests. Of course all this applies to statistical research in other areas of science as well. The pitfalls are manifold and subtle. Unless an experiment can be successfully replicated many times, the results may be nothing more than a statistical anomaly. Extraordinary claims for new laws of science demand extraordinary evidence.

Has extraordinary evidence been provided to support the claim of global warming? The results, from my interpretation of the literature at this time (the reader is encouraged to conduct his or her own investigation and may disagree with my conclusions), is a consistent inconsistency.

HANDPICKED CASES

Because of the difficulties in making accurate a priori predictions (i.e., future predictions), psychics have often relied upon a posteriori interpretations (i.e., attempting to create a plausible explanation for a known outcome) as evidence of supernatural influence. Rephrased, those who believe in the supernatural will find some strange occurrence and create a supernatural explanation as the causal factor (remember, as previously discussed, isolated strange coincidences are normal). In addition to placing these types of handpicked events within the whole context of odds, critical thinkers also look for more parsimonious explanations for these types of events. For example, in 1898, a book called *Futility* was published. This fictional work was about a magnificent Atlantic liner named *Titan* that did not contain enough lifeboats for all the passengers (which was common practice at that time). In the novel, the ship was believed to be "unsinkable." However, the *Titan* sank to the bottom of the sea one April night after being struck by an iceberg (the spring thaw made icebergs a real danger to ships in those days). Of course, the similarities (others exist) between the *Titan* and the *Titanic* (which also sank on an April night) has been used by believers in the supernatural as "proof" of precognition (i.e., the author foresaw the event). While this is a striking case, please note that it is also a handpicked case. For readers interested in the skeptical response to those who believe this case proves paranormal powers exist, I would recommend Martin Gardner's 1998 edition of *The Wreck of the Titanic Foretold?* that places the event in proper context and provides simpler alternative explanations.

One of the most visually powerful pieces of evidence used to illustrate that global warming is occurring are pictures comparing Mount Kilimanjaro from the 1970s and today. As shown in the pictures, the glaciers certainly do appear to be melting. Scientific investigation of the glaciers also shows that they are retreating and will likely disappear soon if current conditions do not change (Thompson et al. 2002). The example of Kilimanjaro is a striking handpicked case often used as "proof" of global warming. However, critical thinking demands that we seek out evidence rather than simply accept claims at face value.

There does seem to be evidence that is inconsistent with the notion that Mount Kilimanjaro's glaciers are melting because of global warming (just as there is evidence inconsistent that the sinking of the *Titanic* was foretold by paranormal powers). First, the ice fields on Kilimanjaro have varied throughout history; they have not simply started to retreat recently (Thompson et al. 2002). Second, the current melting started over a hundred years ago (before global warming was described), and similar patterns have been found on Rwenzori and Mount Kenya (Kaser et al. 2004). Third, the air temperature has remained relatively constant, indicating that other factors are likely causing melting (Kaser et al. 2004). Fourth, tropical glaciers are impacted by a wide variety of inputs (not just air temperature) such as incoming shortwave radiation, precipitation, cloudiness, and air humidity (Kaser 1999). Fifth, historically, Kilimanjaro has had a greater glacier field when temperatures were warmer than in recent times, and within the last hundred years the glaciers have been retreating both during cooler and warmer conditions (Michaels 2004). Sixth, plausible alternatives have been suggested as the causal

factors for the vanishing glaciers on Kilimanjaro. For example, defor-
estation has altered the moisture content of the air blowing up the
mountain (Mason 2003). Kaser and colleagues' research (2004, 336)
says that "climatological processes other than increased air temperature govern glacier retreat on Kilimanjaro." Specifically, they believe
(329) that "[a] drastic drop in atmospheric moisture at the end of the
19th century and the ensuing drier climatic conditions are likely
forcing glacier retreat on Kilimanjaro."

The important issue is not to settle the debate about global
warming but to assert that critical thinking demands and rigorously
evaluates evidence rather than accepting a handpicked event at face
value. Of all the evidence evaluated for this chapter, relying upon Kilimanjaro as "proof" of global warming is by far the weakest and least
compelling. Yet, how many individuals have accepted global warming
as a fact based primarily upon the before and after pictures of Kilimanjaro—which is emotionally very powerful—without seeking additional evidence? Critical thinking requires us to seek additional evidence, which casts substantial doubt on this handpicked evidence.

SUMMARY

In summary, the intent of this chapter was to use the issue of global
warming to illustrate how critical thinking can be inconsistently
applied to differing claims. It has been my experience that many individuals have strong opinions on this topic based primarily upon media
reports, isolated personal experiences, or various types of secondhand
sources. More than any group, we as critical thinkers have consistently emphasized that media reporting is often misleading and is
often not intended to inform the public, and we have encouraged a
rigorous analysis of firsthand sources. Furthermore, if the standards
that we typically apply to evaluating paranormal claims are consistently applied to the theory of global warming, then the case becomes
weaker and cannot be solved without the collection of more data that
is free of methodological concerns and subjective decision making.

Simply put, we would never use such standards as conclusive when evaluating a psychic claim. For example, imagine that we are not debating human influence on global temperatures but evaluating if over the last twenty-five years a psychic changed global temperatures and wanted to be awarded the one million dollar prize from the James Randi Educational Foundation. Assume the psychic's evidence is the current evidence for warming, and that she made an a priori prediction in 1980 that she would warm the earth via psychic powers at the time the scientific consensus determined the earth was going to cool. I would be willing to wager that critical thinking publications would be filled with articles (and rightly so) pointing out methodological concerns with data collection and analysis, inconsistent findings, and problems with relying upon handpicked cases, to name a few topics. And, would a psychic who today claims he can over the next twenty-five years stop further warming from occurring be eligible for the prize? If global warming is a "fact," the answer should be yes. If so, I'll sign up and hope (I'm no psychic) that we experience a period like the one from 1941 to 1980 again (see figure 10.3)!

In all seriousness, this chapter was intended to illustrate—and I hope we all can agree on this—that what should be avoided is a great confidence in one's belief about any issue (the global warming debate provided a contemporary example here) without the benefit of a critical evaluation. In essence, beliefs without a critical inquiry are based upon faith, which is fine in a religious context but has no business within the realm of critical thinking. Moreover, with more data and more precise tools to accurately collect and analyze the data in the future, the case for or against global warming and the impact of human influence on global temperatures should become further clarified. When this occurs, we all should be open to new evidence as it arises. Unfortunately, because of our evolutionary heritage toward strengthening and maintaining beliefs, those with the strongest current opinions on this issue (I'll include myself as one with a current strong opinion) will typically be the least likely to objectively evaluate the forthcoming evidence (see chapter 7). Yet, this would be another example of inconsistent critical thinking.

Finally, I have heard variations of the following argument in regard to global warming, so I will briefly address this issue. One argument says that even if global warming is not occurring or is not substantially influenced by human activity (once again, the two may be largely independent of each other), the attention that is brought to the issue by the media and various scientists is a good thing because it is "the right thing to do" and will result in a cleaner environment (the economic implications of proposed remedies should not be ignored but are beyond the scope of this chapter). Likewise, it's OK to use the worst-case scenario option to exaggerate claims in order to bring awareness to the issue. The "right thing to do" argument (of course, who decides what is the right thing can quickly become a slippery slope) is an advocacy position, and so is focusing on worst-case scenario. If the worst-case scenario is provided when presenting potential outcomes of global warming, so should most likely to occur, and best-case scenario to provide the full range of potential outcomes. I have nothing against advocacy positions when they are presented as such. (I personally advocate regular exercise throughout a person's lifetime.) However, advocacy is not critical thinking. Critical thinking has no bias or agenda and does not tolerate anyone that intentionally misleads, even for the best of reasons. Critical thinking, when applied to evaluating important claims (e.g., both psychic and environmental), is only loyal to ascertaining the truth!

Chapter 11

POLITICS AND INCONSISTENT CRITICAL THINKING

It is a paradoxical truth that tax rates are too high today and tax revenues are too low and the soundest way to raise the revenues in the long run is to cut the rates now.

—President John F. Kennedy (speech to Economic Club
of New York, December 14, 1962)

F ew things can suspend one's basic skepticism like a fair evaluation of political issues (see Einstein, chapter 9). This is especially true for those individuals who have a strong emotional investment in their political views (much like Arthur Conan Doyle had a strong emotional investment in spiritualism). Likewise, politics is an area in which obtaining the "truth" about an issue is often inherently difficult because of the ambiguity of the data, the vast number of variables involved, and the potential for biased information to be purposely presented to influence how we interpret information (i.e., part of playing politics is presenting misleading evidence to further your position). Simply put, in many cases, one cannot run a simple experiment, control a few extraneous variables, and objectively evaluate the results to determine which political claims and beliefs have merit and which do not.

Perhaps because of the inherent ambiguity of politics and political claims, our preexisting views can bias us in a wide variety of ways and make us resistant to objectively evaluating evidence. Here is an example that you can try at home that illustrates how current beliefs can interfere with an objective analysis of evidence. Find a skeptic of the paranormal who also has extremely strong left-leaning political views (simply flip the order of presentation for someone with strong right-leaning views). This exercise will work best if the critical thinker you have identified not only has strong political views but an emotional investment in those views. First, ask her to comment on what she thought of the policies of the Reagan administration during the 1980s (let her speak uninterrupted; this could take a while). Next, ask her what she thought when the First Lady of the United States invited an astrologer into the White House (again, let her speak uninterrupted; this could take a while). At this point, the individual will be providing standards that can be used to test her consistency in evaluating similar evidence. Then, ask her to comment on what she thought of the policies of the Clinton administration during the 1990s (let her speak uninterrupted).

Then comes the specific point of interest. Ask the individual what she thought when the First Lady of the United States invited a "New Age guru" into the White House to help her "channel" with the "spirit" of Eleanor Roosevelt. If your experience is similar to mine, the actions of the First Ladies during the 1980s and 1990s will receive different scrutiny depending upon the preexisting political beliefs of the individual. Double standards are quickly created, evidence can be dismissed out of hand, and rationales as to why one is not as bad as the other often are given. In fact, some readers may be wondering about the source of claims that psychics and New Age gurus were invited into the White House (perhaps with the intent of dismissing particular evidence, depending upon your current political beliefs). The source for both is the *Skeptical Inquirer* (see http://www.csicop.org/si/). For my money, both of these events are *equally* disturbing but are predictably not treated as so by individuals with strong political beliefs because those beliefs bias an objective analysis.

With that in mind, I would like to examine a political claim that has been repeated over the last twenty years by many members of the media and quite a few individuals within academia. I've picked this claim for two reasons. First, it is one of those political claims for which I can actually provide an answer. Second, I have been surprised how many people have uncritically accepted this claim. Perhaps this should not be surprising, since for many claims we do not have the time to demand evidence, and if the claim is already consistent with our beliefs (either puts those we support in a good light or those we oppose in a negative light), we typically do not seek out disconfirming evidence.

So, what is the claim that is still often repeated today in various forms? Here goes: *The tax cuts of the 1980s caused the record federal deficits.* The claim that reducing tax rates will automatically result in greater deficits because less money flows into the federal treasury is routinely repeated (and often the 1980s are used as the example) by politicians and members of the media today. So did reducing tax rates or "tax cuts" *cause* the record deficits?

Before I go on, keep in mind once again that we are much less skeptical of those statements that are consistent with our belief system because of our biased cognitive system (see chapter 7). Thus, for the individual that did not like the policies of the 1980s, he is more likely to accept this statement at face value, as it seems to make sense. Tax rates were reduced, and the deficit did increase in the 1980s, so this must be true. Once again, if there is one issue that all critical thinkers can agree upon, it's that media reports can be very misleading, or just plain false, and we must actively pursue evidence to evaluate the claim.

The purpose of this chapter will be (a) to illustrate the fundamental problem with making a causal statement about what influences receipts (i.e., revenue) to the federal treasury (simply put, a single factor cannot be isolated with such precision to allow causal statements), (b) to bring in expert analysis on this issue (mathematician John Allen Paulos and economist Thomas Sowell), (c) to look at what happened to revenues to the federal treasury from the end of the 1970s through the 1980s (as Sowell notes, these numbers are widely available, as the budget office of the federal government makes the historical tables available to the public; I found the numbers in less than five minutes doing an Internet search), and (d) to provide the causal explanation as to why the deficit increased to record levels.

First, whether a single factor (e.g., lowering or increasing tax rates) has a known or predictable outcome on federal receipts (i.e., money taken into the federal treasury) is not known at this time (I would argue that this will never be known, for the reasons listed below). If this could be known, then predicting future receipts would be a simple job that could be performed with great accuracy. Of course, future predictions are often widely inaccurate and have to be revised many times throughout the year by the federal budget office. This statement (feel free to check the accuracy of previous "estimates" of federal receipts, particularly when tax rates were changed from the previous year) is not meant as a derogatory comment toward those whose job it is to make the predictions but simply illustrates that changes in the tax code and the multiple inputs that can influence receipts can be highly unpredictable (i.e., making causal statements is not possible), and even the best experts cannot state with certainty what will occur.

As a parallel example, let's take another dynamic system, with multiple inputs, that is often highly unpredictable: will a couple divorce or stay married? Of course, there are multiple inputs that could influence this outcome. For example, the couple's life, their financial situation, whether they argue frequently, how similar/dissimilar their personalities are, how they spend money, their jobs, the amount of time they spend together, the influence of family members and friends, whether they have children and if so, how many, the needs of the children, unexpected events (e.g., the death of a child), and religious beliefs. (I could continue, as the potential number of inputs is vast.) Furthermore, these inputs may have different outcomes depending upon the influence of other types of variables. Thus, the influence of variables may interact with other variables and may change with time. For example, amount of time spent together may influence a newly married couple with no children differently than a longer term marriage with five children. Simply put, no credible argument could be made that a single variable can be used to make causal statements and precise predictions about such a complicated dynamic system as the long-term success or failure of a marriage. At best, one can attempt to identify a relation between variables.

Likewise, there are a wide range of factors (e.g., interest rates, natural disasters, demographics of the population, spending habits of the population, technological advances, worker productivity, energy prices, exchange rates, a wide range of governmental regulations, new laws, weather patterns, immigration policies—many more than can possibly be listed here) that can either directly or indirectly influence the receipts taken in by the federal treasury that are independent of our current tax rates (tax rates are simply one input). For example, let's say that the foreign countries that purchase the majority of our exports go into a deep recession. Thus, foreign consumers do not purchase nearly as many products made by American workers. This input, which has nothing to do with tax rates in America, results in American companies reducing their workforce. Of course, this (at least in the short term) increases the unemployment rate and reduces domestic spending, which in turn lowers the overall receipts to the treasury.

For readers who do not like my description, I will refer you to an expert on this issue, John Allen Paulos, who addresses this topic in his must-read book *A Mathematician Reads the Newspaper* (1996). As Professor Paulos correctly points out, there exists an "indeterminate number" of contingencies that can influence receipts, and "their interaction are too complicated to be determined by variation in any single variable such as the tax rate" (21). Once again, the same concept could be applied to whether a couple divorces (i.e., an indeterminate number of contingencies). Interestingly, Paulos's argument was directed at those who argued that lowering tax rates "caused" an increase in federal receipts, as opposed to the current discussion, which is centered on those who believe that lowering the tax rates "caused" an increase in the federal deficient, which is still repeated in the media today whenever the topic of taxes comes up (i.e., "how are you going to pay for that?").

The purpose here is to make the point that the state of the economy and subsequent federal receipts is too complicated a system to allow anyone to say that a single variable "caused" something. (Just so there is no confusion, I am not arguing that lowering tax rates automatically causes an increase in revenues.) At best, one can simply identify historical trends that have occurred after tax rates have been raised or lowered in particular circumstances to identify a "relation" between variables (I will leave that task to the interested reader, as it is beyond the current discussion). Note that the influence of lowering or increasing tax rates in a given set of circumstances is an area of legitimate debate, but making a causal statement because of the interactions among vast numbers of variables is not possible, which is the whole point.

In addition, let's pretend for a moment that we could hold all of the other variables constant except how humans respond to changes in the tax code (this never occurs in reality). This would allow us to test the theory that raising tax rates will automatically increase receipts to the federal treasury, and decreasing tax rates will automatically decrease tax receipts (of course, this can occur). As an example, let's say the federal tax rate in the future on capital gains (i.e., increased value of assets such as stocks) is 25 percent. Thus, for every dollar in profits you make when you SELL an asset, you keep 75 cents. This tax rate will bring in a certain amount of receipts. However, in the following year, the federal tax rate is increased to 99 percent on capital gains with no warning to taxpayers (once again, a theoretical example; taxpayers have historically responded to the anticipation of differing tax rates in real-world settings by altering their behavior). Thus, you will only be able to keep one cent out of every dollar's profit of sold assets. Of course, the response is for virtually everyone to HOLD onto their assets (why would you give them up when you will keep virtually no profits?) once the new tax rate becomes effective, resulting in little money for the treasury (humans have historically altered their behavior in response to new tax codes by adopting strategies to minimize paying taxes). In contrast, imagine the following year, the capital gains tax is set once again at 25 percent (i.e., you can keep 75 cents for every dollar in profit). In this instance, many people sell assets, taking advantage of the change in tax rates, resulting in more overall money to the treasury for that year despite tax rates being substantially lower.

As economist Thomas Sowell (2004a, 240) notes,

> Although it is common in politics and in the media to refer to government's "raising taxes" or "cutting taxes," this blurs a crucial distinction between tax *rates* and tax *revenues*. The government can change tax rates but the reaction of the public to these changes can result in either a higher or a lower amount of tax revenues being collected. Thus references to proposals for a "$500 billion tax cut" or a "$700 billion tax increase" are wholly misleading because all that the government can enact is a change in tax rates, whose actual consequences can be determined only after the fact.

Thus, raising tax rates does not always result in increasing receipts, and lowering tax rates does not always result in fewer receipts (once again, this certainly can occur). Furthermore, the previous example was extreme (increasing tax rates from 25 percent to 99 percent, and then lowering them back to 25 percent). To make matters more complicated, exactly how humans will respond to changing tax rates is often extremely difficult to predict, especially when the changes in tax rates are less extreme than the previous example. For example, would lowering the tax rates from 25 percent to 15 percent or increasing tax rates from 25 percent to 35 percent result in more or less receipts? Not only is your guess as good as mine, but the correct answer likely changes from one time to another based upon the interconnectedness of the indeterminate number of variables that can influence economic activity. Both Professors Paulos and Sowell agree that the economy involves complex reciprocal interactions, not simple one-way causation for only one variable. The media reports assume one-way causation (i.e., tax rates alone determine revenues). Once again as a comparison, this would be like assuming we can make a one-way causation statement as to why couples divorce.

The bottom line of the above argument is simple: One cannot say that the "tax cuts" ("reducing tax rates" is more accurate) of the 1980s "caused" something to happen to federal receipts and subsequently blame the rising deficits on the changes to the tax rates. The complexity of the number of variables that can interact in a wide variety of ways that ultimately affect receipts prohibits any "causal" statement.

Interestingly, up to this point in the discussion about tax rates and federal receipts, no mention has been made about what actually did happen to the amount of money that flowed into the federal treasury. Note that critical thinking, with its evidence-demanding attitude, requires this information because one would assume that if the individual is claiming that lowering tax rates "caused" the rising deficits, at the very least, federal receipts should have noticeably *declined*. Once again, for an expert's perspective, economist Thomas Sowell (1995) notes that this notion that a reduction in tax rates caused the record deficits in the "1980s is easily refuted with widely available official statistics on the federal government's tax receipts, spending, and deficits" (82). As shown in the below table, federal receipts did not decline but increased nicely (well beyond inflation). Thus, the evidence is exactly the opposite of what is being claimed.

Year	Receipts (Millions of Dollars)
1977	355,559
1978	399,561
1979	463,302
1980	517,112
1981	599,272
1982	617,766
1983	600,562
1984	666,486
1985	734,088
1986	769,215
1987	854,353
1988	909,303
1989	991,190

Source: *Budget of the United States Government: Historical Tables* (Washington, DC: US Government Printing Office, 2005), p. 22, http://www.budget.gov/budget

It is illogical to make the case that increasing the amount of receipts to the federal treasury was the cause of the record deficits. One would have expected, in order to believe that the "tax cuts" of the 1980s caused the record deficits, at least some evidence that tax receipts noticeably declined. They did not. I like to think about the numbers in the previous table as a salary (mine has never come close to those numbers, but one can dream). With that in mind, how could an individual making $909,303 in 1988 have a greater debt at the end of the year (just for that year) than the same individual making $517,112 in 1980? Rephrased, how can someone making substantially more money, well beyond inflation, wind up with a greater debt? Perhaps the below table will solve the mystery (once again, this information is widely available).

The answer to the great mystery of what "caused" the record deficits (at least at that time) is simple: The federal government spent much more money than it took in. It is no more complicated than

Year	Receipts (Millions of Dollars)	Outlays (Money Spent; Millions)	Deficit (Millions of Dollars)
1977	355,559	409,218	− 53,659
1978	399,561	458,746	− 59,185
1979	463,302	504,028	− 40,726
1980	517,112	590,941	− 73,830
1981	599,272	678,241	− 78,986
1982	617,766	745,743	−127,977
1983	600,562	808,364	−207,802
1984	666,486	851,853	−185,367
1985	734,088	946,396	−212,308
1986	769,215	990,441	−221,227
1987	854,353	1,004,083	−149,730
1988	909,303	1,064,481	−155,178
1989	991,190	1,143,813	−152,623

Source: *Budget of the United States Government: Historical Tables* (Washington, DC: US Government Printing Office, 2005), p. 22, http://www.budget.gov/budget

that. In fact, spending almost doubled from 1980 to 1988. While receipts during the 1980s showed a healthy increase (for whatever reason; once again, a causal statement is not possible), it simply could not keep up with spending. There is no evidence that the reduction in tax rates caused the rising deficits, unless the individual wants to claim that more money alone causes greater deficits. If that is the case, how many of us would volunteer to take less money from their employer in order to reduce debt? None!

Now, for the individual who wants to debate what the money should or should not have been spent on, go right ahead, as that is an area of legitimate debate (large increases for entitlements and military spending appear to be the two largest increases according to the Federal Budget Office). However, the illusion that we can say with certainty that the deficits in the 1980s were caused by lower tax rates or "tax cuts," as the media likes to say, should be a dead issue. Yet, this issue persists in modern political debates, which are typically devoid of evidence, and uncritical acceptance of information is common. Of course, to the true believer, no amount of evidence can change one's belief system (e.g., Einstein and Conan Doyle), and I do not anticipate this chapter will change the views of anyone with strong political beliefs.

Chapter 12

MULTICULTURAL CLAIMS

Are Skeptics Sexist and Racist?

Statistical comparisons implicitly assume that the groups being compared are indeed comparable on the relevant variables. Very often, however, they are not even close to being comparable.
—Thomas Sowell, *The Quest for Cosmic Justice* (2002a, p. 35)

N o one would deny that discrimination (e.g., racism, sexism) exists. The most qualified applicant for the job who is not hired for the position because of her race is the classic example of overt discrimination. A "softer" form of discrimination also exists. For example, take a college professor who typically provides students with rigorous feedback and sets high standards for student achievement in an attempt to help students maximize their potential. However, for students of a certain race, gender, age, physical appearance, and so on, the professor (for whatever reason, and it may be a conscious or unconscious process) does not give those students the same feedback and sets lower standards. In this scenario, the "soft" discrimination may result in a lesser educational experience that will ultimately put that student at a disadvantage later on. In any case, discrimination occurs in a variety of ways and to a variety of groups and individuals and should not be tolerated.

With that in mind, there is a widespread belief in many academic and intellectual circles that statistics that show disparities (i.e., unequal outcomes based upon the assumption of equal representation) between groups provide strong evidence of discrimination. This belief is particularly prevalent within many "politically correct" circles, which provide no compelling evidence to support this claim (as well as many other claims) but instead prefer to bully individuals by branding them, or threatening them, with a derogatory label that could damage their reputation (nobody wants to be labeled a racist and/or sexist). Furthermore, the argument claims that if the statistics indicate disparities, the burden of proof should be shifted to the accused to demonstrate they are not engaged in discriminatory practices. Unfortunately, when this technique is used against some individual, group, institution, company, organization, and so on that we personally despise (think of an example here before proceeding), our critical thinking about the quality of the evidence can be suspended. Why question evidence that is consistent with our preexisting beliefs? It is easy to say, "I knew he was a racist or sexist all along," and now the "evidence" proves it! Numbers don't lie! However, the standards of critical thinking do not care about our personal feelings or preexisting beliefs but demand evidence seeking and a rigorous evaluation of the quality of the evidence. Thus, critical thinking demands an inquiry into the claim that statistical discrepancies can "prove" discrimination.

As an example (assume for this example you personally hate this company because you despise its owner), let's say in one part of the country, the local community was made up of 50 percent purple people and 50 percent blue people (the actual races for the example are irrelevant). Imagine, however, that a particular company's workforce was made up of 85 percent blue people and 15 percent purple people. Because a substantial intergroup disparity exists (i.e., there is not an equal amount of blue and purple consistent with what would be expected in the population), the conclusion is compelling evidence of discrimination against the purple people. Rephrased, a case of discrimination is made based simply upon gross numbers, and the burden of proof is then shifted to the accused to prove themselves innocent (once again, when we despise the accused, it's easy to accept this as evidence). Of course, the company could be discriminating, but are we ready to accept statistical disparities as proof without any other type of evidence to support the claim? Unfortunately, many do. (Some members of the Supreme Court believe in this argument; I'll leave it to the reader to discover which members.)

However, there are several problems with this type of statistical approach. First, the individual must assume that the groups being compared are equivalent on all the remaining relevant variables. However, the statistical data alone do not provide enough information on such relevant variables as experience, age, education, self-selection, interest in that particular type of work, worker performance, absenteeism, worker attitudes, and so forth that are necessary to make comparisons meaningful. Simply put, from a research perspective, confounding variables are not controlled, making the statistics meaningless (statistics cannot rescue a poor research design, which is exactly the case here). In reality, often the groups being compared are not equivalent on the relevant variables, and sometimes there are gross differences between the groups on very pertinent variables.

Second, the statistical approach assumes that in a discrimination-free environment groups will be proportionally represented. However, as Sowell (1995) has noted, "international studies have repeatedly shown gross intergroup disparities to be commonplace all over the world" (35). As one example that you can try in your local community, calculate the number of male and female kindergarten teachers in your local school district (typically female-dominated). Likewise, calculate the number of male and female T-ball coaches (typically male-dominated). Both groups work with five- to six-year-olds. If there is equal representation, then your community is the exception, not the rule. Is discrimination the likely culprit or is there another relevant variable, such as self-selection? The statistical approach says discrimination, particularly if the outcome is consistent with a prevailing belief. However, "a reasonably comprehensive listing of such disparities would be at least as large as a dictionary" (Sowell 1995, 35).

As further evidence that disparities are the rule, not the exception, statistical disparities should not exist in favor of groups who are in no position to discriminate (and have often been discriminated against), such as minority groups and women. Interestingly, Sowell (see *Migrations and Cultures, The Quest for Cosmic Justice, The Vision of the Anointed, Applied Economics*) has compiled a vast list of these types of disparities in which it is virtually impossible to claim the disparities are due to discrimination because they favor groups in no position to discriminate against others. As a few examples, (a) women in the United States are six times less likely to be struck by lightning than men (are storm clouds sexist?), (b) Germans made up about 40 percent of czarist Russia's high army command, despite being approximately 1 percent of the population (i.e., a minority group), (c) people of Japanese ancestry produce about 90 percent of the tomatoes in São Paulo, Brazil, (d) people of Cambodian ancestry own more than 80 percent of the doughnut shops in California, (e) Jews, despite making up less than 1 percent of the world's population, have been awarded more than one-third of the Nobel prizes in economics, (f) 80 to 90 percent of all university students in engineering, science, and medicine in Malaysia during the 1960s were from the Chinese minority, and (g) African Americans are "overrepresented" in such sports as professional basketball and professional football. The list could go on, and on, and on (like the Energizer bunny).

As further examples that large statistical disparities are commonplace, let's take a quick look at Mother Nature. As someone who lives in the Buffalo, New York, area (specifically, Grand Island), I can attest to the fact that Mother Nature typically over-represents us with too much snow during the winter. However, compared with other states, we also have an overabundance of fresh water available from the Great Lakes. Colorado has many mountains with peaks over fourteen thousand feet high. In contrast, Kansas, located right next to Colorado, has none. Seattle, Washington, has its fair share of rain, while the city of Los Angeles would probably like a bit more. I could continue with international examples, but I believe the point has been made. Simply put, disparities are commonplace not only among humans, but in nature as well.

As Sowell (2002) notes, "Why are different groups so disproportionately represented in so many times and places? Perhaps the simplest answer is that there was no reason to have expected them to be statistically similar in the first place. Geographical, historical, demographic, cultural, and other variables make the vision of an even or random distribution of groups one without foundation" (37). While there is no denying discrimination exists, relying upon this type of statistical approach, simply showing disparities and shifting the burden of proof to the accused while ignoring social, economic, and cultural patterns of various ethnic and racial groups is methodologically unsound (confounding variables are not controlled) and based upon a false assumption (i.e., equal representation would automatically occur in a discrimination-free environment). Yet, how many of us would suspend our critical thinking (the author has done this in the past) and simply accept the statistical approach as strong evidence without a skeptical inquiry if we learned the accused was somebody we reviled?

With that basic information in mind, let's assume (just for fun) that we accept the belief that statistical disparities can demonstrate that an individual company or organization discriminates and we believe that if disparities are shown, the burden of proof should be shifted to the accused to prove themselves innocent. Once again, this argument is easy to accept at face value when it is selectively applied in the courtroom to some person or group we already dislike (our pre-existing beliefs can influence our critical thinking).

Let's turn the tables on ourselves for a moment by applying that standard (statistical disparities alone can prove discrimination) to ourselves. So, what does the evidence show about statistical disparities for critical thinkers and skeptical groups? Do we possess equal representation? In Prometheus Books' "science and paranormal section" in the 2001 spring-summer catalog (note that Prometheus Books, the publisher of this book, is a leading publisher of books related to critical thinking), David Myers (2002) counted 110 male authors and only 4 female authors. The reader can obtain an updated count at www .prometheusbooks.com, although nothing substantial has changed as of this writing. As another example, the fellows of the Committee for

Skeptical Inquiry (CSI) are dominated by men. Also, I believe that the members of this organization also have great intergroup disparities when it comes to racial makeup. As yet another example, in browsing through the editorial board of *Skeptic* magazine (published by the Skeptics Society), I see that there are similar intergroup disparities among the members. In fact, groups that promote critical thinking across the board show unequal disparities. Carl Sagan (1996) has noted that these discrepancies are obvious at gatherings of critical thinkers.

So, what are we to make of ourselves? Are we part of groups that are practicing discriminatory policies? Are skeptics as a group sexist and racist? Should groups that promote critical thinking be forced to prove their innocence, which could cost a substantial amount of money in litigation and potentially bankrupt some of the smaller organizations? Just so there is no confusion about my personal belief here, I do not think that critical thinkers and skeptical organizations are any more (or any less, for that matter) racist/sexist than the general population. The important issue is how we are sometimes vulnerable to apply different standards of proof and evidence to evaluate different claims. It's easy to accept this claim at face value when it is directed at this company or that organization (particularly if it is consistent with our preconceived notions of such groups), but it's not so easy to apply the same standards to ourselves. Humans have a well-documented tendency to exclude ourselves from the standards we set for others, another factor that can in some instances contribute to us being inconsistent critical thinkers.

Chapter 13
ECONOMISTS AND SKEPTICS
Birds of a Feather?

But the near-universal acceptance of a belief does not prove that it is valid or even meaningful any more than the general belief in witches or ghosts proved the validity of these concepts.
—Economist F. A. Hayek, *Law, Legislation and Liberty,*
volume 2 (1976, p. 66)

L et's say for a moment that you have a friend who is a highly respected economist, an extremely bright individual, an analytical thinker who possesses critical thinking skills, and so on. However, your friend does not possess basic knowledge about the history of skepticism and the methods of skepticism as they pertain to the evaluation of psychics. Rephrased, your friend, while having many positive attributes, has not taken the time to familiarize himself with the specifics of skepticism. At this point, would you feel comfortable in letting that individual evaluate a psychic for the one million dollar prize offered by the James Randi Educational Foundation (www .randi.org)? More than likely, the answer is no. He may not realize that psychics have a history of attempting to cheat during evaluations (this information is key to control for that possibility), he likely would not secure the help of conjurers for the evaluation to identify any magic tricks, he may not be familiar with the specific methods necessary (e.g., double-blind, controlling for a placebo effect) to evaluate a psychic claim, and so on. In short, people are at a disadvantage when venturing outside of their specific field, especially when they have not taken the time to familiarize themselves with the basics of skepticism.

Now, let's turn the tables. Imagine you have a friend who is a highly respected skeptic, an extremely bright individual—all positive characteristics are the same as in the previous example. However, the skeptic has not taken the time to familiarize herself with economics. At this point, how much confidence you have in your friend's ability to evaluate a politician's claim on an economic topic? I personally would have as much confidence in the skeptic's ability to evaluate an economic claim as I would in the economist's ability to evaluate a psychic claim for the same reasons listed above. Interestingly, unlike such fields as psychology, biology, and physics, economics has been virtually ignored in the skeptical literature, or is often presented with equal time with someone who has an opposing view (an unusual standard). The purpose of this chapter is (a) to point out some consistencies that exist between both skeptics and economists, and (b) to try to persuade the critical thinker who is vocal with political issues of the importance of economic knowledge (remember Asimov's endorsement of a doomsday prediction from the introduction?). In fact, I believe the reader will find that economists sometimes have the same complaints (i.e., widespread uncritical acceptance of information) and make many of the same arguments as the critical thinker! As an example, see economist Julian Simon's interview by *Skeptic* (Miele 1997).

A BASIC UNAWARENESS OF SKEPTICISM AND ECONOMICS

Skeptics have long argued that many individuals are misinformed or uninformed about issues related to paranormal phenomena, which may help to explain why beliefs in the paranormal are so widespread. Rephrased, many people believe in paranormal phenomena (e.g., the Bermuda Triangle) because they have not taken the time to become fully informed on an issue and simply have relied upon either personal experiences or anecdotal secondhand information.

Furthermore, the skeptical literature is littered with cases of scientists and other intellectuals who lack the basic skills and knowledge required to appropriately evaluate and test psychic claims (see chapter 2). Unfortunately, scientists' pronouncements even on issues in which they possess no expertise are often accompanied by the aura of credibility. Thus, the pronouncements of the authenticity of "psychics" by a scientist can have great weight with the general public. Of course, the classic example is the scientist (or anyone, for that matter), who lacks knowledge of basic conjuring skills and subsequently evaluates a psychic. More often than not, the psychic simply uses some basic magic tricks, but the scientist is fooled and claims that he has witnessed "true" psychic occurrences; these pronouncements add to the misinformation (Randi 1982). For example, scientist Charles Richet was fooled by several psychic mediums who used simple conjuring techniques during séances. And, as previously mentioned (see chapter 8), Mina Crandon (aka Margery) fooled many within the scientific community and was on the verge of being labeled "genuine" by *Scientific American*. The potential number of examples that could be provided here is vast.

Economists have long voiced similar concerns that virtually everyone has an opinion on economic matters (typically based on personal experience or secondhand anecdotes), but few have taken the time to familiarize themselves with basic economic principles. Likewise, many scientists (and other intellectuals) who lack basic knowledge of economics or skills to evaluate economic claims, have long voiced their opinions on economic matters with the authority of a scientist (Hayek 1991; Simon 1999; Sowell 1995). Albert Einstein provides an example of a scientist who admittedly was not an expert on economic issues (Einstein 1950) and who did not hesitate to comment on economic matters (see following for an example), but who was one of many scientists that talked "much nonsense on economic matters" (Hayek 1991, 60). In fact, many examples exist where scientists have looked as foolish commenting on economic matters as some scientists have evaluating psychics, particularly when they lack even basics economic knowledge (economist Julian Simon's books are filled with wonderful examples). Moreover, some scientists "go so far as to tell economists that their discipline is fundamentally wrong and they do not understand their own subject matter" (Simon 1999, 62). Can you imagine a musician, with expertise in playing the violin, telling a brain surgeon that she does not understand her subject matter?

There have been repeated predictions over the years that the earth was nearing the end of some natural resource (this can occur in an abstract sense, but the real issue is whether or not the resource is nearing total depletion). Note that varying "experts" have been predicting that the earth is running out of oil for decades. Here are a few examples provided by economists Maurice and Smithson (1984, quoted from p. 13) in their book *The Doomsday Myth: 10,000 Years of Economic Crises*:

1891   The U.S. Geological Survey predicted that there was little or no chance of finding oil in Texas.

1926   The Federal Oil Conservation Board predicted the United States had only a seven-year supply of petroleum remaining. Senator LaFollette predicted that the price of gasoline would soon rise to $1 per gallon.

1939   The Interior Department predicted that U.S. petroleum supplies would last for less than two decades.

1949   The Secretary of the Interior predicted that the end to U.S. supplies of oil was almost in sight.

Likewise, economist Thomas Sowell (1995) notes that a best-selling book in 1960 (Vance Packard's *The Waste Makers*) predicted that the United States only had a thirteen-year supply of oil left if consumption remained constant. Interestingly, the petroleum reserves in the 1960s were about thirty-two billion barrels, but in 1973 the reserves were more than thirty-six billion barrels. What happened? Why do these types of predictions, much like psychic predictions, have such poor accuracy over the years? Can knowledge and expertise from economists inform us as to why we should be skeptical of such predictions?

Economists point out that there is a substantial difference between *actual reserves* (how much really exists) and *known reserves* (how much we have discovered at this point) of natural resources. The predictions that we are "running out" treat known reserves as if they are actual reserves (see Sowell 2004a for a more detailed discussion). In fact, nobody knows how much actual reserves of a natural resource like oil exist. Previous estimates by "experts" have been so widely inaccurate that they do not even provide a reasonable estimate. It is the present value that affects both the use and the discovery of natural resources, which impacts known reserves. Simply put, there are many economic factors that go into how profitable it would be to discover how much of the supply actually exists. As Simon (1990, 87) nicely articulates:

> Known reserves are much like the food we put into our cupboards at home. We stock enough groceries for a few days or weeks—not so much that we will be carrying a heavy, unneeded inventory that ties up an unnecessary amount of money in groceries, and not so little that we may run out if an unexpected event, such as a blizzard, should descend upon us. The amount of food in our cupboards tells little or nothing about the scarcity of food in our communities, because it does not as a rule reveal how much food is available in the retail stores. Similarly, the oil in the "cupboard"—the quantity of known reserves—tells us nothing about the quantities of oil that can be obtained in the long run at various costs. This explains why the quantity of known reserves, as if by a miracle of coincidence, stays just a step ahead of demand.

The previous predications (all were wrong, by the way) that we are at the end of the earth's oil supplies did not make the simple distinction between actual and known reserves. Of course, we may be nearing the end of some types of natural resources, but that would imply that all actual reserves have been discovered and become known reserves. Those who have not taken the time to learn this simple distinction have made many blunders in evaluating the state of natural resources over the years. Interestingly, despite massive oil use around the world, the known reserves of the world were more than ten times as large at the end of the twentieth century as they were in the middle of the century (Sowell 2004a). Nobody knows how much actual oil exists. Perhaps we have found all of the oil, but perhaps not.

Likewise, many individuals (some scientists included; most notably Stanford biologist Paul Ehrlich) have made a variety of "doomsday predictions" over the years that failed to take into account several basic economic principles that would have been useful to consider (Maurice and Smithson 1984; Simon 1999). Typically, the predictions are made by extrapolating existing short-term trend lines out into the future. As Sowell notes (1995, 68), "Extrapolations are the last refuge of a groundless argument. In the real world, everything depends on where we are now, at what rate we are moving, in what direction, and—most important of all—what is the specific nature of the process generating the numbers being extrapolated." As an example, imagine that a couple decides to wait until marriage to have sexual relations, and the courtship lasts a year. Then, extrapolate the number of times the couple will have sexual intercourse into the future based upon the short-term trend that occurs during the honeymoon. It does not take much of an extrapolation before the couple is having sex hundreds of times a day. Other such extrapolations can be equally as meaningless but are often the supporting evidence for future predictions. Of course, extrapolations of short-term trends are useful for selling books and gaining media attention (doomsday stories, like stories about the paranormal, sell more books and have higher ratings on television), but they have not been an effective tool for making accurate future predictions.

Also, extrapolations of this sort assume that humans do not adapt their behavior to changing situations. This assumption is simply false and not supported by any meaningful evidence. Once again, think about amount of sexual activity for a couple on their honeymoon and that same couple ten years later with three young children who do not sleep through the night. Most couples (perhaps all) respond to the changing situation. As an example with economic implications, let's assume that the current price of a pack of cigarettes is $3 (this includes tax). Imagine, overnight, the State of New York increased the taxes on cigarettes so that a pack now costs $20. Does anyone want to argue that human behavior will not adapt to the changed "here and now"? Some likely changes would be that some people would decide that cigarettes are too expensive and either stop smoking or drastically reduce the amount they smoke. Others, if they live near Indian reservations—which sell tax-free cigarettes—will purchase their cigarettes there to avoid or minimize the taxes. Likewise, those near the Canadian border will start to frequent the duty-free shops, or cross over to neighboring states to purchase cigarettes. In addition, black markets are likely to spring up for those without the option to avoid the increased taxes, and so forth. In short, humans adapt to changing situations. (In Buffalo, we put on shorts and T-shirts in the summer, and coats and hats in the winter!)

Furthermore, doom merchants fail to take into account that shortages result in price increases (Maurice and Smithson 1984). Price increases also impact human behavior (e.g., they consume less, they substitute alternative products), which once again makes the extrapolations poor future predictors. Likewise, doom merchants fail to consider the impact of technological development (so, too, did Thomas Malthus, whose overpopulation doomsday prediction was wrong yet still widely accepted by many today). As an example of substituting an alternative product in response to rising prices, the oil we use today is in response to the whale oil crises that occurred in the 1850s (see Maurice and Smithson 1984). People used to light lamps and lubricate machinery with whale oil, but rising prices resulted in a new product (today's oil) being substituted for the old product (whale oil). In fact, one of the major assumptions made in these types of doomsday predictions, which are inconsistent with the facts of human history, is that humans have no creative spark to increase productivity or develop alternative products but are simply inert (Simon 1990). This assumption seems extremely peculiar today, given that we are in an age of science and that technological advances are a regular part of our culture. Apparently, scientists, inventors, and entrepreneurs have no more benefits to produce for humans. The list could go on, but the doom merchants have a track record comparable with psychic predictions over the years because their testing procedures are suspect and they ignore or are unaware of basic economic principles.

As one last example, Paul Ehrlich, in the prologue to his book *The Population Bomb* (1968, xi), makes the following statement, "The battle to feed all of humanity is over. In the 1970's the world will undergo famines—hundreds of millions of people are going to starve to death." This statement was accompanied by recommendations for compulsory population control and was flat-out wrong. In fact, Ehrlich has made a career out of making very speculative predictions (e.g., he would bet even money that England would not exist in the year 2000; we are running out of oil) that have one thing in common with religious apocalyptics' and Nostradamus's end-of-the-world predictions: they never come true (Simon 1999). What is interesting, however, is that being wrong with such great consistency has failed to hurt Ehrlich's scientific reputation, as he was rewarded for his failed predictions by winning a MacArthur Foundation "genius" grant. As Sowell (1995) correctly points out, "Paul Ehrlich is perhaps preeminent for having been wrong by the widest margins, on the most varied subjects—and for maintaining his reputation untarnished through it all" (67). For example, Ehrlich is still given space in such prestigious journals as *Science* on the very topic of future predictions (see Ehrlich and Kennedy 2005).

THE IMPORTANCE OF EVALUATING CLAIMS

At the heart of skepticism is the belief that claims should be evaluated and that the evidence—not any individual's preexisting beliefs—should win out. Of course, in evaluating the claim that psychic powers exists, one can never with exact certainty exclude the possibility that psychic powers exist in other individuals or other circumstances. Thus, even if a psychic fails a specific test, one can never say with 100 percent certainty that there is no such thing as psychic powers. However, skeptics tend to look for a consistency in the pattern of results to make evaluations. (Note that cases of random chance also need to be ruled out; thus, isolated cases that have not been replicated are not viewed as compelling evidence.) As it currently stands, under double-blind conditions, the results are extremely consistent: no genuine case of psychic abilities has yet been demonstrated (Riniolo and Schmidt 1999a).

Likewise, economics is concerned with the empirical evaluation of the effectiveness of various policies and economic actions on the efficient allocation of scarce resources, as opposed to the goals of policies. Thus, economics also believes in the evaluation of claims and that it is the evidence that should win out, not what an individual would like to happen. Specifically, the effectiveness of policies that influences the quality and standard of living for millions of individuals is something economists are interested in evaluating. For example, Albert Einstein, in an article originally published in the first issue of *Monthly Review* (*Why Socialism?* May 1949; see Einstein 1950, for a reprint of the article), advocates a planned economy (i.e., central planning). Albert Einstein is the classic example of a scientist who repeatedly ventured outside his area of expertise while not even attempting to learn the basics of the discipline in which he would subsequently make public comments. This claim (i.e., the effectiveness of central planning) has been subsequently evaluated.

After fifty-plus years of data, in which many countries implemented various forms of central planning, the results around the world "turned out to be worse than anyone expected" (Sowell 2004, 18), and the problems that hampered the effectiveness of central planning were seen in both democratic societies (e.g., India) and totalitarian societies (e.g., USSR, China). As one example, many countries that used to export food now had to import food to feed their populations. Perhaps the most striking example comparing a centrally planned economy with a free market economy, as pointed out by Nobel Prize–winning economist Milton Friedman (1994, xiv), was the distinction between East and West Germany. "Here are people of the same blood, the same civilization, the same level of technical skill and knowledge, torn asunder by the accidents of warfare, yet adopting radically different methods of social organization—central direction and the market. The results are crystal clear. East Germany, not West Germany, had to build a wall to keep its citizens from leaving. On its side of the wall, tyranny and misery; on the other side, freedom and affluence."

Consistent findings exist when comparing other similar populations such as North Korea/South Korea, China/Hong Kong, and China/Taiwan (Simon 1990). Even communist governments (e.g., China) have begun to abandon the disastrous results of central planning. The evidence clearly does not support the belief that central planning results in a better quality of life for individual citizens. (Although beyond the discussion here, the notion that an "intellectual elite" can dictate what job the individual must perform should be frightening to anyone who values personal freedom.) Perhaps central planning works in some isolated context (perhaps psychic powers exist in some isolated context), but the empirical evidence that central planning results in a lower standard of living than market economies is overwhelming. (Note that in 1987, only 60 percent of housing facilities in East Germany had indoor toilets compared with 95 percent in West Germany; see Simon 1990 for other examples.) Yet, how many people still preach the virtues of central planning? Perhaps it's just me, but I like having the freedom to pursue the occupation of my choosing, and I have a real fondness for indoor toilets!

SKEPTICS AND ECONOMISTS AS "DEVILS"

Psychics (and many in the media) have long portrayed themselves as being on the side of the "angels," while those nasty skeptics are nothing more than "devils" (John Stossel is one notable exception of a media person who does not present skeptics in this manner). Psychics seek to have evaluations focus on superficial results (i.e., feelings and emotional responses) and want to focus on lofty goals instead of a rigorous evaluation of evidence. Also, psychics typically do not want any evaluation of the long-term consequences. For example, a "faith healer" may treat any individual for a genuine physical illness, such as cancer (you have seen the faith healers on late-night cable channels, where people go up on stage and are "healed"). The evidence that the psychic wants to rely upon is how the individual "feels" after the treatment (usually some laying of hands on the person), not with the actual effectiveness of the treatment and the long-term ramifications of the treatment. Unfortunately, many individuals with treatable illnesses who have relied upon faith healers have gone home to die because they temporarily felt better (i.e., a placebo effect) and believed they were cured. Of course, the skeptic is not only concerned about this method of evaluation (i.e., relying upon short-term feelings), but the long-term consequences that can accompany this type of psychic healing. Unfortunately, the long-term consequences, as just mentioned, are typically very sad.

Economics has been labeled the dismal science, perhaps because economists, like skeptics, do not want to rely upon "lofty goals" and short-term "feelings" but are likewise interested in the long-term impacts of specific policies. Also, economics, like skepticism, has often been viewed as "narrow," particularly when evaluating claims that someone has their heart set on. For example, let's take a politician who is advocating "rent control" to make housing "affordable" for her city. Who does not want affordable housing? In this scenario, the media typically interviews, in the short run, those selected individuals who would benefit from a government-mandated lowering of rent. Typically, anyone objecting to this type of policy is not presented in the best light (i.e., on the side of the devils) by the media. Again, who could be against such a lofty goal as affordable housing?

The economist, however, like the skeptic, is interested not only in the short-term but in the long-term consequences of the policy. Just like the faith healer, the politician has typically moved on and does not wait for the long-term implications. Worldwide, when rent control has been implemented, the long-term consequences have included shortages (supply decreases while demand increases; also, more housing is occupied by single renters, further exacerbating the problem), declines in quality (e.g., it becomes unnecessary for owners to maintain a high-quality product to sell because of the great demand; likewise, some buildings are simply abandoned by the owners if rent-control policy forces losses on the property), black markets occur, to name a few of the long-term negative consequences (see Sowell 2004, 2004a for further discussion). Once again, humans adapt behavior to changing circumstances. Thus, while rent control sounds wonderful, the long-term consequences worldwide have been much different than what those who advocate the policy have told people will happen. Of course, when economists point this out, they are typically dismissed as the bad guys, like the skeptic who points out that the faith healer is selling snake oil.

MYTHS AND MISPERCEPTIONS

Many myths and misperceptions are perpetuated in the general public that critical thinkers know are false and thus are easy to spot. For example, the "curse of King Tut" is a myth that states that anyone who entered the tomb of the Egyptian king Tutankhamen was subsequently cursed and would die an early death. As Randi (1997) notes, the curse is simply an "international myth started by the press and carefully nurtured by them ever since" (236). Even empirical evaluations (see Nelson 2002; Randi 1997) of the life expectancy of those exposed to the "curse" have done little to disprove the myth. Likewise, despite media reports, there is nothing special about the Bermuda Triangle (see Randi 1982 for further details). Countless other examples of perpetuated myths exist, but those without expertise or familiarity with the skeptical literature are less likely to spot a myth or misconception and will repeat or uncritically accept the misinformation in the future.

Likewise, for those unfamiliar with the economics literature, there are just as many myths and misperceptions that continue to be perpetuated. For example, there is no such thing as the trickle-down theory of economics, which has been typically perpetuated as a description of some of the economic policies of the 1980s. Within politics and the media, this terminology is still used, but it reflects a lack of even the basic understanding of economics. Specifically, "trickle-down" has implied that benefits must first be given to the "rich" or "big business," then the benefits will eventually trickle down to the masses. However, "no recognized economist of any school of thought has ever had any such theory or made any such proposal. It is a straw man. It cannot be found in even the most voluminous and learned histories of economic theories" (Sowell 2004a, 388). Workers are the first to be paid, not the business owners or the investors who are taking a risk with their money (just the opposite of "trickle-down"). Simply put, profits flow up, not down (often profits never occur, as many businesses fail). As Sowell points out, the popular online bookstore Amazon.com began operations in 1994 but did not turn its first profit until 2001. Yet the workers were paid, even when the company was losing quite a bit of money, and there was never a guarantee it would ever turn a profit (how many dot-com companies went bankrupt, and how many investors lost their money?). Many additional examples could be given (the "rich" and "poor" are static groups, free-market economists are simply pro-business apologists, economic activity is a zero-sum process with solely winners and losers). Once again, without knowledge of economics, the individual is much more likely to accept and repeat what are no more than simple myths and misconceptions.

DON'T ALL ECONOMISTS DISAGREE?

I anticipate that some will dismiss this chapter with the following argument: economics is a discipline in which everyone disagrees, so learning about economics is solely a matter of opinion and thus of little relevance for the critical thinker. First, that is similar to the same argument that psychics have been using for years to dismiss scientific evaluations (i.e., scientists disagree about the possibility of supernatural occurrences, so let's just ignore all scientific opinion on the topic and go with our feelings and emotional responses). Second, there is at

least as much agreement (perhaps more agreement) among economists when compared with psychologists, so the contributions from
psychologists to the critical thinking community would likely have to
be abandoned as well, using that logic. As Sowell (2004a) correctly
points out, "While there are controversies in economics, as there are
in science, this does not mean that economics is just a matter of
opinion. There are basic propositions and procedures in economics
on which a Marxist economist like Oskar Lange did not differ in any
fundamental way from a conservative economist like Milton
Friedman" (4).

In this chapter, I simply relied upon basic economic principles
with widespread agreement (e.g., known reserves differ from actual
reserves, central planning failed, rent-control policies have failed),
and tried to reinforce the notion of the importance of learning more
about a specific topic prior to having great confidence in our beliefs.
For those interested in learning more about economics, please refer
to Sowell's *Basic Economics* and *Applied Economics*, which were written
for the general public and are a nice place to start for learning about
a topic that influences our lives but about which we often have strong
opinions based upon surprisingly little evidence beyond our own isolated personal experiences or what we would like to be true.

Chapter 14

DOES SANTA CLAUS UNDERMINE CRITICAL THINKING?

No, No, No

The stockings were hung by the chimney with care,
In hopes that Saint Nicholas soon would be there.
> —*The Night before Christmas*

During the fall of 1897, eight-year old Virginia O'Hanlon wrote a letter to the editor of the *New York Sun*, asking, "Is there a Santa Claus?" The response, published on September 21 (originally unsigned, but now widely credited to Francis P. Church), is the now famous "Yes, Virginia, There Is a Santa Claus" editorial, which is widely available on the Internet (see http://www.newseum.org/yesvirginia/). Interestingly, undermining skepticism was one of the major themes in the "Yes, Virginia" editorial.

Over the years I have been asked a variation of Virginia O'Hanlon's question by students who know that I am a skeptical college professor with children. Specifically, students have asked if I teach my own children the Santa myth. Many seem surprised when I tell them yes. Perhaps they associate those who advocate critical thinking with the Grinch! Santa Claus has over the years been linked to undermining critical thinking skills in our society by some critical thinkers. However, like many parents, I find the Santa myth to have a positive message on balance (i.e., being good for goodness's sake) and want to promote long-lasting positive memories. Moreover, I believe the Santa issue can be discussed here to illustrate inconsistent standards, and a credible argument can be made that perpetuating the Santa myth provides many children with the first great skeptical experience of their lives. In contrast, the argument that Santa has long-term negative consequences is a weak argument at best and is not based upon any compelling evidence at this time (perhaps some will be forthcoming in the future).

Before we continue, it is important to point out that perhaps this chapter is (once again) nothing more than the author's own biases (both emotional and cognitive) showing through, so let me disclose them now. Some of my fondest childhood memories are of the Christmas season, particularly those having to do with Santa Claus. Yes, we watched "Rudolph the Red-Nosed Reindeer" every Christmas (I still watch it during the holiday season). Likewise, we left out cookies and milk for Santa and carrots for the reindeer on Christmas Eve. The anticipation of Christmas morning and the presents that Santa would leave is a wonderful and enduring set of personal memories that influence my thinking. Thus, my parents perpetuated the Santa myth. Likewise, with my own children, my wife (who is equally fond of Santa) and I both have continued the tradition. I must say that we find sharing the whole Santa experience with the children equally satisfying. Thus, I am writing this chapter with the clear bias that I like Santa and make no apologies for this viewpoint. However, it is not my intention to tell any parent what customs and traditions are suitable for your family (you know your family and children better than I do) but to use this issue to illustrate inconsistent critical thinking and why the claims sometimes thrown out about Santa are not consistent with critical thinking.

With that disclaimer in hand, I would like to address the following issue that has been repeated by various critical thinkers in talks and in book form (as one example, see Tom Flynn's *The Trouble with Christmas*, 1993). Specifically, some critical thinkers have made variations of the following claim over the years: It's not surprising that so many people do not think critically and believe in nonsense when we teach our own kids about Santa. Thus, Santa is linked to a variety of unwanted causal outcomes. For example, as Flynn (1993) notes, "What price are we paying for lying to children about Santa Claus? It may be steeper than we think. Because the myth panders to childhood credulity, some have implicated it in the rising incidence of scientific illiteracy among the young. Because it encourages children to build their world views on authority, not on independent thinking, others have related it to the abysmal judgment supposedly displayed in young adults" (148). Interestingly, when these types of claims are made (Santa linked to scientific illiteracy or foolish decisions made by adolescents), critical thinkers have traditionally not required any evidence to support the claim. (I know of no time when such claims have been required to provide a shred of credible evidence.)

Several problems exist with this interpretation of linking Santa as a causal variable for noncritical and nonscientific thinking. First, there is no evidence to support such claims. These types of claims fall under the category of extraordinary claims. We like to say "extraordinary claims require extraordinary evidence," so let's see the evidence (a rigorous scientific investigation). None exists. The claim is made, without any supporting evidence, and the burden of proof is on the person making the speculative claim. Here, so there is no confusion, the speculative claim is that perpetuating the Santa myth leads to a lifetime of noncritical thinking or has increased the amount of noncritical thinking in today's society.

Second, these claims ignore the law of parsimony (see chapter 3). There are many other simpler explanations as to why scientific illiteracy may be rising or why young adults may make poor decisions. For example, compared with adults, many young adults process more information in the limbic system, and less in the frontal lobe. The frontal lobe is the portion of the brain that allows us to make logical and rational decisions. Likewise, humans possess a wide variety of cognitive biases that can undermine our ability to think critically (a more parsimonious explanation). In addition, parents, teachers, and school systems obviously play a vital role in a child's education and the development of critical thinking skills. (If Santa does play a larger role than the just-mentioned variables, then the education of a child really is in jeopardy.) If Santa was purged from the culture at large, and everything else remained the same, no evidence exists to suggest that this would lead to a society of critical thinkers, as cultures that do not perpetuate Santa do not have advanced numbers of critical thinkers. In addition, historically, before the Santa myth became widespread, there was no evidence that superstitious beliefs and behaviors were not widespread (remember witches?). I could continue, but I believe the point is made that simpler explanations must be ruled out prior to making a causal statement about Santa and the lack of critical thinking in today's society.

Third, let me provide a ridiculous claim for comparison against the Santa-undermines-critical-thinking claim. Specifically, I will claim that perpetuating the Santa Claus myth is a causal variable for adults later making important scientific discoveries. (Just so there is no confusion, I do not believe this, but I do believe that the critical thinker would demand evidence and rigorously evaluate evidence for this silly claim.) What's my evidence you ask? Well, countries in which the "Santa myth" is part of the larger cultural experience are dominant in scientific discoveries. I'll take the United States, Germany, and England as my top three picks (all perpetuate Santa, as do many other scientifically advanced nations). You can choose your top three non-Santa countries, and then let's make a list. Anyone want to bet that mine will be "nice" and yours "naughty"? Of course, this silly claim also ignores more parsimonious explanations as to why some countries may be more scientifically productive than others. Why would this claim be rigorously challenged, yet when Santa is haphazardly linked to some negative outcome with no credible evidence to support the claim, the same standards of evidence are ignored? Once again, inconsistent critical thinking.

Likewise, I am sure the argument I am about to make (and perhaps the one I just made) can be vulnerable to the charge of inconsistency as well. However, let's concentrate now on why there is perhaps an additional bonus for perpetuating the Santa myth (i.e., how Santa can actually provide a positive skeptical experience) for those critical thinkers who do carry on the cultural tradition. Prior to addressing that issue, some background information is necessary.

BACKGROUND INFORMATION:
MAGICAL THINKING IN CHILDREN

At approximately age three, a paradoxical coexistence of two differing types of thought processes begins to emerge in the preschool child. First, young children start to develop sophisticated thinking capabilities about causal mechanisms and normal events (Chandler and Lalonde 1994; Johnson and Harris 1994; Phelps and Woolley 1994). Thus, young children can be viewed as naive scientists who begin trying to discover how the world works by testing theories in physics, biology, and psychology (Rosengren and Hickling 2000; Rosengren, Kalish, Hickling, and Gelman 1994). For example, children gain an understanding that nonliving objects do not spontaneously appear or disappear, that physical growth occurs from small to large (e.g., kitten to cat), and objects fall to the ground.

Paradoxically, a belief in "magical thinking" coexists that gives rise to (a) paranormal explanations of natural processes (i.e., the magnets attracting or repelling are caused by "real" magic), and (b) a belief in the reality of fantasy figures (e.g., monsters, Santa Claus, Tooth Fairy). Even very young children start to develop skepticism about magic and magical figures once they establish the causal relation or understand that the event is a normal process (Woolley, Phelps, Davis, and Mandell 1999). In addition, as children's knowledge of causal mechanisms and natural processes increases, the use of magical explanations decreases. For example, Phelps and Woolley (1994) report that 75 percent of four-year-olds believe that a magician's magic is real (should magicians be banned as well as Santa?), contrasted with 12 percent of eight-year-olds. Likewise, children's beliefs in the efficacy of wishing declines substantially with age (Woolley, Phelps, Davis, and Mandell 1999).

It has only been within the past fifteen years that researchers have started to investigate the role of magical thinking and how magical beliefs influence children's searching for causal understanding. First, evidence shows the dominant mode of thinking in children is scientifically oriented and constrained by physical, psychological, and biological laws (Rosengren and Hickling 2000). Thus, the early theory proposed by Piaget (1929) that children's thinking processes are primarily magically oriented is inconsistent with current empirical evidence. Thus, when the child is pretending that a cardboard box is really a pirate ship or a race car, the child knows the difference between reality and fantasy. However, magical thinking is a normal part of cognitive development (even for children who have never heard of Santa) and is itself part of our evolutionary heritage. The interesting question for further discussion here is: if childhood thought is not dominated by magical thinking, then what role does magical thinking play?

Current research suggests that magical thinking occurs when an event violates the child's expectations and the child lacks a natural explanation. Thus, "Preschoolers may begin to recruit alternative causal models, especially magical beliefs, for those circumstances that violate their now rich causal-explanatory beliefs" (Rosengren and Hickling 2000, 81). Magical explanations serve a useful purpose in helping children to "preserve rather than undermine their commitment to systems of natural law" (Chandler and Lalonde 1994, 84). In essence, magical thinking is a natural part of cognitive development with the purpose of allowing the child to compartmentalize contradictory evidence without threatening their entire belief system. For example, when the child witnesses a direct violation to a well-established principle (e.g., objects are supposed to roll downhill), labeling a visual illusion (i.e., an object appearing to roll uphill) as a real magical event allows the child to maintain the physical principle without abandoning his entire belief system, until further understanding of how the world works occurs. Thus, contemporary theory and research results support the notion that magical thinking plays an important role in supporting, not undermining, scientifically oriented thinking in children.

Finally, for completeness, Subbotsky (2000) has proposed an interesting theory in which the coexistence of scientific and magical thinking exists throughout the entire lifespan in a permanent fight for dominance. His theory provides a framework to explain not only why some individuals are more prone to paranormal explanations but why even very scientifically oriented individuals can, under selected circumstances, invoke a magical explanation or demonstrate behavior consistent with magical thinking (e.g., the scientist who is also a sports fan who wears his "lucky" hat during the game). In addition, magical thinking is seen worldwide in every culture, which helps to support the belief that it is a universal trait in humans.

THE SANTA MYTH AS A POSITIVE SKEPTICAL EXPERIENCE

One way to teach critical thinking is to create exercises in which the individual can practice the process of skeptical thinking and generate their own conclusions based upon the evidence. The primary argument presented in this chapter is that during the childhood years, there is no single better event to allow children to practice critical thinking than discovering the truth of the Santa myth on their own, as most children do between the ages of six and eight years old (Anderson and Prentice 1994).

Note that the Santa myth is perpetuated not only by parents and other family members but by the culture at large (e.g., television, songs, strangers, movies, teachers). When children first develop an understanding of Santa in the preschool years, they believe the reality of the fantasy figure (i.e., magical thinking) because they lack the cognitive development necessary to challenge the myth. Thus, the Santa myth is a culturally perpetuated myth that lasts for years and is initially automatically believed without any skeptical evaluation because the understanding of causal mechanisms and normal events necessary to challenge the magical explanation is lacking. Furthermore, the Santa myth is not only long lasting but represents a highly cherished belief (who does not love presents?).

Over the years, however, the child continues to develop a sophisticated knowledge base and understanding of causal mechanisms and normal events while continuing to believe in Santa. Eventually, cognitive development reaches a point at which the magical explanation (i.e., Santa is real) is confronted with the child's increasing understanding of the world. As previously mentioned, the dominant thinking mode in children is scientifically oriented (Rosengren and Hickling 2000; Rosengren, Kalish, Hickling, and Gelman 1994). Thus, a longstanding, highly cherished belief starts to become questioned.

After the first seeds of doubt occur, most children perform a skeptical inquiry in trying to determine the reality of Santa Claus. For example, children start to ask critical questions (e.g., How could Santa possibly visit every house in one night? Why are people shopping for presents if Santa brings the toys? How come the reindeer at the zoo can't fly? Why did Santa wrap the presents with the same paper that mommy bought at the store?), gather evidence (e.g., survey and question classmates, older children, and adults about Santa), and develop alternative hypotheses (e.g., Could some or all presents be coming from alternative sources besides Santa?) prior to eventually discovering the truth.

Simply put, the Santa myth is a useful event for children to practice critical thinking on a widespread, culturally perpetuated myth. While other events occur that allow children to practice critical thinking, no other single event of such personal importance exists (i.e., children want Santa to be real) for which children so actively seek to find the truth. Is that not what critical thinking is all about? Also, the Santa myth is user-friendly with no major negative side effects (compare believing in Santa to having gotten caught up in believing in "repressed memories"; see Loftus and Ketcham 1994). First, the Santa myth does not spin out of control, leading to a lifetime of magically oriented thinking but is compartmentalized (just like other magical beliefs, such as believing that a magician has real magical powers) until the child discovers the truth. Second, the majority of children report positive reactions after discovering the truth (Anderson and Prentice 1994). Some within the "psychobabble crowd" also disapprove of Santa, without a shred of evidence to support their speculative claims that Santa somehow permanently damages the bonds between parent and child. In fact, knowing I am on the opposite side of the psychobabble folks leads me to believe that I am on the right track in being pro-Santa!

Perhaps one of the great challenges to promoting critical thinking is the development of more user-friendly "Santa-like" investigative exercises at different stages of the lifespan to reinforce the importance of critically evaluating our own cherished beliefs. Carl Sagan (1996) has recommended applied exercises to teach scientifically oriented thinking, and allowing children to skeptically evaluate the Santa Claus claim accomplishes that goal. However, a wide range of exercises with varying outcomes would help to reinforce that critical thinking is a process of gathering and evaluating evidence, not simply a debunking technique.

CONCLUSIONS

While many legitimate reasons exist for not perpetuating the Santa myth to a child (that decision should be left to the child's parents or caregiver), the rationale that Santa undermines critical thinking is inconsistent with the argument presented in this chapter. Unfortunately, there is an absence of long-term studies that have investigated the consequences for perpetuating the Santa myth in childhood and how that may influence critical thinking later in life. Based upon the limited evidence presented in this chapter, I would predict that there is no negative relation between the variables because (a) magical thinking in childhood is part of the normal developmental process in learning how the world works, and (b) contemporary theory believes and supporting evidence indicates that it serves the very useful purpose of promoting scientifically oriented thinking by allowing the child to compartmentalize isolated inconsistencies without threatening the whole belief structure.

Thus, perhaps the real magic of Santa Claus is his creating an opportunity for children to discover that sometimes the world is not as it first appears, and Santa's real gift to children is one much greater than any toy: providing a user-friendly event to practice the process of critical thinking. However, if that interpretation is simply wishful thinking (it may be), there still exists not a single shred of credible evidence that Santa causes widespread negative outcomes that undermine critical thinking and that banishing him (I suppose you would also have to banish other cultural traditions, certain books, certain movies, magicians, etc.) would lead to an increase in our society's critical thinking. Thus, I will challenge those making the claim to provide the evidence, just as critical thinkers have correctly challenged those who believe that distant prayer results in healing to provide the evidence. At this time, none exists. So, until such evidence is provided, as Santa would say, "A Merry Christmas to all, and to all a good night."

Conclusion

CLOSING THOUGHTS

Visions may be moral, political, economic, religious, or social. In these or other realms, we sacrifice for our visions and sometimes, if need be, face ruin rather than betray them.
—Thomas Sowell, *A Conflict of Visions* (2002, p. xii)

So, what should the reader take away from this book? First, I hope the reader has gained an appreciation that there can in certain contexts exist a difference between the critical thinker's ability (i.e., the evidence-demanding attitude and method of inquiry) and performance (i.e., objectively implementing skeptical skills). Our beliefs can interfere with our critical thinking performance because we all are biased toward strengthening and maintaining our current beliefs (both true and false beliefs), especially those beliefs that we value. From an evolutionary standpoint, this book has hypothesized that these biases were advantageous to maximize the benefits from our pattern-seeking abilities and to keep our pattern seeking from undermining our beliefs, which eventually would decrease the evolutionary advantage by reducing the likelihood that humans would act on information. Thus, our pattern-seeking heritage became interconnected with our biased cognitive system. However, today our cognitive and emotional biases directly influence our beliefs, and those beliefs can directly influence our own individual critical thinking performance without our conscious knowledge.

Thus, if the reader takes one lesson from this book, I hope it is that due diligence is required to minimize the influence of our beliefs from interfering with our ability to apply critical thinking to evaluate a wide range of claims. A development of self-awareness that in certain situations we may all abandon (or have previously abandoned) our critical thinking skills in order to maintain our beliefs, especially our precious beliefs, is an important component to making us, critical thinkers, ultimately better performers. As previously shown, even such brilliant thinkers as Isaac Asimov (see introduction) and Albert Einstein (see chapter 9) were not immune from the influence of their evolutionary heritage. If it could happen to them, it seems likely it can happen to any of us.

In addition, this book was also intended for those who are beginning to learn about critical thinking and to point out the benefits of critical thinking as ultimately the best way to develop an informed opinion and rigorously evaluate evidence. Thus, when a new claim comes along or if we wish to evaluate our current beliefs, critical thinking is the single best method to determine the accuracy of the claim. Why else would anyone advocate critical thinking? The standards of critical thinking require that we should be asking exactly what the evidence is, we should not be relying upon secondhand sources, we should seek out expert help when necessary, we should seek out or implement double-blind studies when possible and actively pursue parsimonious explanations first, and so on. Critical thinking is not only essential for evaluating paranormal claims or other speculative types of claims but any claim of importance in our lives (e.g., buying a house). Thus, an important goal for all of us is to maximize our critical thinking across a wide range of important claims.

Finally, I am hoping this book will encourage other critical thinkers to take an interest in the topic of inconsistent critical thinking (i.e., performance not matching ability). We should never assume that our critical thinking skills make us immune from uncritical acceptance of information, and this point should be reinforced every now and again in publications for the critical thinker and in the classroom by those who teach courses that stress critical thinking. While continual refinement of our critical thinking skills is important and should be encouraged, *perhaps equally important is strengthening our capacity to use our current ability in a more consistent manner*.

Furthermore, this book has encouraged the development of a greater self-awareness as a good first step to limit inconsistent critical thinking. Yet, situations exist in which we are unaware that we are not critically evaluating information. Thus, I would encourage others with an interest in this topic to think about developing some formalized steps or procedures that may be useful to ensure that performance closely approximates critical thinking ability.

Finally, while this book has focused on the cognitive biases that contribute to our potential for abandoning or inconsistently applying our critical thinking under certain conditions, there likely exist multiple inputs that contribute for each individual, such as social and motivational factors. Thus, additional inputs should also be explored. Likewise, this book has focused on critical thinking as it pertains primarily to the evaluation of claims, but the influence of our beliefs on other aspects of critical thinking should also receive attention (e.g., logic, problem solving). For the critical thinker, one of our most precious beliefs may be that we could not possibly believe in nonsense (that belief is comforting). I hope this book has provided the reader enough evidence to challenge that belief, or at least to consider the argument presented.

REFERENCES

Abbey, A. 1982. Sex differences in attributions for friendly behavior: Do males misperceive females' friendliness? *Journal of Personality and Social Psychology* 42:830–38.

Anderson, C. A., and K. L. Kellam. 1992. Belief perseverance, biased assimilation, and covariation detection: The effects of hypothetical social theories and new data. *Personality and Social Psychology Bulletin* 18:555–65.

Anderson, C. J., and N. M. Prentice. 1994. Encounter with reality: Children's reactions on discovering the Santa Claus myth. *Child Psychiatry and Human Development* 25:67–84.

Applebaum, A. 2004. *Gulag: A history*. New York: Anchor Books.

Balling, R. C., Jr. 2005. Observational surface temperature records versus model predictions. In *Shattered consensus: The true state of global warming*, ed. P. J. Michaels, 50–71. Lanham, MD: Rowman & Littlefield Publishers.

Balling, R. C., Jr., P. J. Michaels, and P. C. Knappenberger. 1998. Analysis of winter and summer warming rates in gridded temperature time series. *Climate Research* 9:175–81.

Barber, T. X. 1976. *Pitfalls in human research: Ten pivotal points*. New York: Pergamon Press.

Bem, D. J., and C. Honorton. 1994. Does psi exist? Replicable evidence for an anomalous process of information transfer. *Psychological Bulletin* 115:4–18.

Born, M. 1971. *The Born-Einstein letters*. Trans. Irene Born. New York: Macmillan Press.

Bornstein, R. F. 1990. Manuscript review in psychology: An alternative model. *American Psychologist* 45:672–73.

Braithwaite, R. J. 2005. Glacier mass balance, the first 50 years of international monitoring. *Progress in Physical Geography* 26:76–95.

Bratman, S. 2005. The double-blind gaze: How the double-blind experimental protocol changed science. *Skeptic* 11:64–73.

Braun, K. A., R. Ellis, and E. F. Loftus. 2002. Make my memory: How advertising can change our memories of the past. *Psychology and Marketing* 19:1–23.

Burton, G. 2001. The tenacity of historical misinformation: Titchener did not invent the Titchener illusion. *History of Psychology* 4:228–44.

Campbell, D. T., and J. C. Stanley. 1963. *Experimental and quasi-experimental designs for research*. Chicago: Rand McNally College Publishing Company.

Caute, D. 1988. *The fellow-travellers: Intellectual friends of communism*. Rev. ed. New Haven, CT: Yale University Press.

Cerveny, R. S. 2005. Severe weather, natural disasters, and global change. In *Shattered consensus: The true state of global warming*, ed. P. J. Michaels, 106–20. Lanham, MD: Rowman & Littlefield Publishers.

Chandler, M. J., and C. E. Lalonde. 1994. Surprising, magical and miraculous turns of events: Children's reactions to violations of their early theories of mind and matter. *British Journal of Developmental Psychology* 12:83–95.

Christopher, K. 2003. The ABC-ville horror. *Skeptical Inquirer* 27:53–54.

Christy, J. R., R. W. Spencer, and W. D. Braswell. 2000. MSU tropospheric temperatures: Dataset construction and radiosonde comparisons. *Journal of Atmospheric and Oceanic Technology* 17:1153–70.

Christy, J. R., D. J. Seidel, M. Cai, E. Kalnay, C. K. Folland, C. A. Mears, P. W. Thorne, and J. R. Lanzante. 2006. What kinds of atmospheric temperature variations can the current observing systems measure and what are their strengths and limitations, both spatially and temporally? In *Temperature trends in the lower atmosphere: Steps for understanding and reconciling differences*, ed. T. R. Karl, S. J. Hassol, C. D. Miller, and W. L. Murray, 29–46. Washington, DC: Climate Change Science Program and the Subcommittee on Global Change Research.

Cialdini, R. B. 2001. *Influence: Science and practice*. 4th ed. Needham Heights, MA: Allyn & Bacon.

Collacott, E. A., J. T. Zimmerman, D. W. White, and J. P. Rindone. 2000. Bipolar permanent magnets for the treatment of chronic low back pain. *Journal of the American Medical Association* 283:1322–25.

Comiso, J. C. 2000. Variability and trends in Antarctic surface temperatures from *in situ* and satellite infrared measurements. *Journal of Climate* 13:1674–96.

Darley, J. M., and P. H. Gross. 1983. A hypothesis-confirming bias in labeling effects. *Journal of Personality and Social Psychology* 44:20–33.

Darwin, C. 1859/2003. *The origin of species*. New York: Signet Classic.

———. 1874/1998. *The descent of man*. 2nd ed. Amherst, NY: Prometheus Books.

Dineen, T. 1998. Psychotherapy: The snake oil of the 90s? *Skeptic* 6:54–63.

Ditto, P. H., and D. F. Lopez. 1992. Motivated skepticism: Use of differential decision criteria for preferred and nonpreferred conclusions. *Journal of Personality and Social Psychology* 63:568–84.

Doran, P. T., J. C. Priscu, W. B. Lyons, J. E. Walsh, A. G. Fountain, D. M. McKnight, D. L. Moorhead, R. A. Virginia, D. H. Wall, G. D. Clow, C. H. Fritsen, C. P. McKay, and A. N. Parsons. 2002. Antarctic climate cooling and terrestrial ecosystem response. *Nature* 415:517–20.

Doyle, A. C. 1992. *The coming of the fairies*. London: Holder and Stoughton.

Easterling, D. R., B. Horton, P. D. Jones, T. C. Peterson, T. R. Karl, D. E. Parker, M. J. Salinger, V. Razuvayev, N. Plummer, P. Jamason, and C. K. Folland. 1997. Maximum and minimum temperature trends for the globe. *Science* 277:364–67.

Edwards, K. 1990. The interplay of affect and cognition in attitude formation and change. *Journal of Personality and Social Psychology* 59:202–16.

Ehrlich, P. R. 1968. *The population bomb*. New York: Ballantine.

Ehrlich, P. R., and D. Kennedy. 2005. Millennium assessment of human behavior. *Science* 309:562–63.

Einstein, A. 1949. *The world as I see it*. Trans. Alan Harris. New York: Wisdom Library.

———. 1950. *Out of my later years*. New York: Philosophical Library.

Ellenberger, H. F. 1972. The story of "Anna O.": A critical review with new data. *Journal of the History of the Behavioral Sciences* 8:267–79.

Ericsson, K. A., and N. Charness. 1994. Expert performance: Its structure and acquisition. *American Psychologist* 49:725–47.

Fabrigar, L. R., and R. E. Petty. 1999. The role of the affective and cognitive bases of attitudes in susceptibility to affectively and cognitively based persuasion. *Personality and Social Psychology Bulletin* 25:363–81.

Fancher, R. E. 1996. *Pioneers of psychology*. 3d ed. New York: W. W. Norton.

Fernald, D. 1984. *The Hans legacy: A story of science*. Hillsdale, NJ: Lawrence Erlbaum Associates.

Flynn, T. 1993. *The trouble with Christmas*. Amherst, NY: Prometheus Books.

Fox Kane, M. 1888/1985. Spiritualism exposed: Margaret Fox Kane confesses to fraud. In *A Skeptic's Handbook of Parapsychology*, ed. P. Kurtz. Amherst, NY: Prometheus Books.

Friedman, M. 1994. Introduction to F. A. Hayek, *The road to serfdom*. 50th Anniversary ed. Chicago: University of Chicago Press.

Gardner, M. 1998. *The wreck of the Titanic foretold?* Amherst, NY: Prometheus Books.

Garzke, W. H., Jr., D. K. Brown, A. D. Sandiford, J. Woodward, and P. K. Hsu. 1996. The *Titanic* and *Lusitania*: A final forensic analysis. *Marine Technology* 33:241–89.

Gilovich, T. 1993. *How we know what isn't so: The fallibility of human reason in everyday life*. New York: Free Press.

Glaser, R., and M. T. H. Chi. 1988. Overview. In *The nature of expertise*, ed. M. T. H. Chi, R. Glaser, and M. J. Farr. Hillsdale, NJ: Erlbaum.

Glenn, N. D. 1991. The recent trend in marital success in the United States. *Journal of Marriage and the Family* 53:261–70.

Goldstein, I., T. F. Lue, H. Padma-Nathan, R. C. Rosen, W. D. Steers, and P. A. Wicker. 1998. Oral sildenafil in the treatment of erectile dysfunction. *New England Journal of Medicine* 338:1397–1404.

Greenwald, A. G., E. R. Spangenberg, A. R. Pratkanis, and J. Eskenazi.1991. Double-blind tests of subliminal self-help audiotapes. *Psychological Science* 2:119–22.

Gross, P. R., and N. Levitt. 1998. *Higher superstition: The academic left and its quarrels with science*. Baltimore, MD: Johns Hopkins University Press.

Hamilton, D. L., and T. L. Rose. 1980. Illusory correlation and the maintenance of stereotypic beliefs. *Journal of Personality and Social Psychology* 39:832–45.

Hansel, C. E. M. 1961. A critical analysis of the Pearce-Pratt experiment. *Journal of Parapsychology* 25:87–91.

Haselton, M. G., D. M. Buss. 2000. Error management theory: A new perspective on biases in cross-sex mind reading. *Journal of Personality and Social Psychology* 78:81–91.

Hayek, F. A. 1944/1994. *The road to serfdom*. 50th Anniversary ed. Chicago: University of Chicago Press.

————. 1952/1976. *The sensory order: An inquiry into the foundations of theoretical psychology.* Chicago: University of Chicago Press.

————. 1976. *Law, legislation and liberty, vol. 2: The mirage of social justice.* Chicago: University of Chicago Press.

————. 1991. *The fatal conceit: The errors of socialism.* Chicago: University of Chicago Press.

Heckhausen, J. 2001. Adaptation and resilience in midlife. In *Handbook of Midlife Development*, ed. M. E. Lachman, 345–94. New York: Wiley.

Hines, T. 2002. A Classic in Skeptical History. In *The Skeptic Encyclopedia of Pseudoscience (vol. 2)*, ed. M. Shermer, 822–23. Santa Barbara, CA: ABC-CLIO.

Hojat, M., J. S. Gonnella, and A. S. Caelleigh. 2003. Impartial judgment by the "gatekeepers" of science: Fallibility and accountability in the peer review process. *Advances in Health Sciences Education* 8:75–96.

Hook, S. 1987. *Out of step: An unquiet life in the 20th century.* New York: Harper & Row.

————. 2002. *Sidney Hook on pragmatism, democracy, and freedom: The essential essays.* Ed. R. B. Talisse and R. Tempio. Amherst, NY: Prometheus Books.

Houdini, H. 1924. *Houdini exposes the tricks used by the Boston medium "Margery."* New York: Adams.

————. 1924/1972. *Houdini: A magician among the spirits.* New York: Arno Press.

Hunter, G. W. 1914. *A civic biology.* New York: American Book Company.

Hyman, R. 1994. Anomaly or artifact? Comments on Bem and Honorton. *Psychological Bulletin* 115:19–24.

Isbister, J. N. 1985. *Freud: An introduction to his life and work.* Cambridge, England: Polity Press.

Jacobson, J. W., J. A. Mulick, and A. A. Schwartz. 1955. A history of facilitated communication: Science, pseudoscience, and antiscience. *American Psychologist* 50:750–65.

Jelalian, E., and A. G. Miller. 1984. The perseverance of beliefs: Conceptual perspectives and research developments. *Journal of Social and Clinical Psychology* 2:25–56.

Johannessen, O. M., K. Khvorostovsky, M. W. Miles, and L. P. Bobylev. 2005. Recent ice-sheet growth in the interior of Greenland. *Science* 310:1013–16.

Johnson, C. N., and P. L. Harris. 1994. Magic: Special but not excluded. *British Journal of Developmental Psychology* 12:35–51.

Johnston, L. 1996. Resisting change: Information-seeking and stereotype change. *European Journal of Social Psychology* 26:799–825.

Joughin, I., and S. Tulaczyk. 2002. Positive mass balance of the Ross Ice Streams, west Antarctica. *Science* 295:476–80.

Kalnay, E., and M. Cai. 2003. Impact of urbanization and land-use change on climate. *Nature* 423:528–31.

Kaplan, S., and R. S. Kaplan. 1995. *The Amityville horror conspiracy*. Lacyville, PA: Belfrey Books.

Kaser, G. 1999. A review of the modern fluctuations of tropical glaciers. *Global and Planetary Change* 22:93–103.

Kaser, G., D. R. Hardy, T. Mölg, R. S. Bradley, and T. M. Hyera. 2004. Modern glacier retreat on Kilimanjaro as evidence of climate change: Observations and facts. *International Journal of Climatology* 24:329–39.

Keene, M. L. 1997. *The psychic mafia*. Amherst, NY: Prometheus Books.

Klaus, M. H., R. Jerauld, N. C. Kreger, W. McAlpine, M. Steffa, and J. H. Kennell. 1972. Maternal attachment: importance of the first postpartum days. *New England Journal of Medicine* 286:460–63.

Kurtz, P. 1985. *A skeptic's handbook of parapsychology*. Amherst, NY: Prometheus Books.

Lanzante, J. R., T. C. Pteerson, F. J. Wentz, K. Y. Vinnikov, D. J. Seidel, C. A. Mears, J. R. Christy, C. E. Forest, R. S. Vose, P. W. Thorne, and N. C. Grody. 2006. What do observations indicate about changes of temperatures in the atmosphere and at the surface since the advent of measuring temperatures vertically? In *Temperature trends in the lower atmosphere: Steps for understanding and reconciling differences*, ed. T. R. Karl, S. J. Hassol, C. D. Miller, and W. L. Murray, 47–70. Washington, DC: Climate Change Science Program and the Subcommittee on Global Change Research.

Laqueur, W. 1990. *Stalin: The glasnost revelations*. New York: Charles Scribner's Sons.

Larson, E. J. 1998. *Summer for the Gods: The Scopes trial and America's continuing debate over science and religion*. New York: Basic Books.

Lepper, M. R., L. Ross., and R. R. Lau. 1986. Persistence of inaccurate beliefs about the self: perseverance effects in the classroom. *Journal of Personality and Social Psychology* 50:482–91.

Levinson, D. J., C. N. Darrow, E. B. Klein, M. H. Levinson, and B. McKee. 1978. *The seasons of a man's life*. New York: Knopf.

Loftus, E. F. 2003. Make-believe memories. *American Psychologist* 58:867–73.

Loftus, E. F., and K. Ketcham. 1994. *The myth of repressed memory*. New York: St. Martin's Press.

Loftus, E. F., and J. E. Pickrell. 1995. The formation of false memories. *Psychiatric Annals* 25:720–25.

Lord, C., L. Ross, and M. Lepper. 1979. Biased assimilation and attitude polarization: The effect of prior theory on subsequently considered evidence. *Journal of Personality and Social Psychology* 37:2098–2109.

Mahoney, M. J. 1976. *The scientist as subject: The psychological imperative*. Cambridge, MA: Ballinger Publishing Company.

———. 1977. Publication prejudices: An experimental study of confirmatory bias in the peer review system. *Cognitive Therapy and Research* 1:161–75.

———. 1985. Open exchange and epistemic progress. *American Psychologist* 40:29–39.

———. 1987. Scientific publication and knowledge politics. *Journal of Social Behavior & Personality* 2:165–76.

Mahoney, M. J., and B. G. DeMonbreun. 1977. Psychology of the scientist: An analysis of problem-solving bias. *Cognitive Therapy and Research* 1:229–38.

Marshall, B. J., and J. R. Warren. 1984. Unidentified curved bacilli in the stomach of patients with gastritis and peptic ulceration. *Lancet* 8390:1311–15.

Mason, B. 2003. African ice under wraps. *Nature* online publication. http://www.nature.com/nsu/031117/031117-8.html.

Masson, J. M. 1985. *The complete letters of Sigmund Freud to Wilhelm Fliess, 1887–1904*. Cambridge, MA: Harvard University Press.

Maurice, C., and C. W. Smithson. 1984. *The doomsday myth: 10,000 years of economic crises*. Stanford, CA: Hoover Institution Press.

McKendry, I. G. 2003. Applied climatology. *Progress in Physical Geography* 27:597–606.

Mears, C. A., C. E. Forest, R. W. Spencer, R. S. Vose, R. W. Reynolds, P. W. Thorne, and J. R. Christy. 2006. What is our understanding of the contribution made by observational or methodological uncertainties to the previously reported vertical differences in temperature trends? In *Temperature Trends in the Lower Atmosphere: Steps for Understanding and Reconciling Differences*, ed. T. R. Karl, S. J. Hassol, C. D. Miller, and W. L. Murray, 71–88. Washington, DC: Climate Change Science Program and the Subcommittee on Global Change Research.

Micceri, T. 1989. The unicorn, the normal curve, and other improbable creatures. *Psychological Bulletin* 105:156–66.

Michaels, P. J. 2004. *Meltdown: The predictable distortion of global warming by scientists, politicians, and the media.* Washington, DC: Cato Institute.

———. 2005. Introduction. False impressions: Misleading statements, glaring omissions, and erroneous conclusions in the IPCC's summary for policymakers, 2001. In *Shattered consensus: The true state of global warming,* ed. P. J. Michaels, 1–19. Lanham, MD: Rowman & Littlefield Publishers.

Michaels, P. J., and R. C. Balling Jr. 2000. *The satanic gases: Clearing the air about global warming.* Washington, DC: Cato Institute.

Michaels, P. J., P. C. Kanppenberger, R. C. Balling Jr., and R. E. Davis. 2000. Observed warming in cold anticyclones. *Climate Research* 14:1–6.

Miele, F. 1997. Living without limits: An interview with Julian Simon. *Skeptic* 5:54–59.

Milton, J., and R. Wiseman. 2001. Does psi exist? Lack of replication of an anomalous process of information transfer. *Psychological Bulletin* 127:434–38.

Mitroff, I. I. 1974. Norms and counter-norms in a select group of the Apollo moon scientists: A case study of the ambivalence of scientists. *American Sociological Review* 39:579–95.

———. 1974a. *The subjective side of science: A philosophical inquiry into the psychology of the Apollo moon scientists.* Amsterdam, The Netherlands: Elsevier Scientific Publishing Company.

Moseley, J. B., K. O'Malley, N. J. Petersen, T. J. Menke, B. A. Brody, D. H. Kuykendall, J. C. Hollingsworth, C. M. Ashton, and N. P. Wray. 2002. A controlled trial of arthroscopic surgery for osteoarthritis of the knee. *New England Journal of Medicine* 347:81–88.

Myers, D. 2002. The power of coincidence. *Skeptic* 9:28.

Myers, D. G. 2002. *Intuition: Its powers and perils.* New Haven: Yale University Press.

———. 2005. *Social psychology.* 8th ed. New York: McGraw-Hill.

Nelson, M. R. 2002. The mummy's curse: Historical cohort study. *British Medical Journal* 325:1482–84.

Nickell, J. 2003. Amityville: The horror of it all. *Skeptical Inquirer* 27:13–14.

Ofshe, R., and E. Watters. 1994. *Making monsters: False memories, psychotherapy, and sexual hysteria.* Berkeley: University of California Press.

Parkinson, C. L. 2002. Trends in the length of the southern ocean sea-ice season, 1979–99. *Annals of Glaciology* 34:435–40.

Paulos, J. A. 1996. *A mathematician reads the newspaper*. New York: Anchor Books.

Pendergrast, M. 1996. *Victims of memory: Sex accusations and shattered lives*. 2nd ed. Hinesburg, VT: Upper Access Publishing.

Pennebaker, J. W., and J. A. Skelton. 1978. Psychological parameters of physical symptoms. *Personality and Social Psychology Bulletin* 4:524–30.

Phelps, K. E., and J. D. Woolley. 1994. The form and function of young children's magical beliefs. *Developmental Psychology* 30:385–94.

Piaget, J. 1929. *The child's conception of the world*. London: Routledge & Kegan Paul.

Polidoro, M. 2001. *Final séance: The strange friendship between Houdini and Conan Doyle*. Amherst, NY: Prometheus Books.

———. 2002. The search for Margery. *Skeptical Inquirer* 26:19–21.

Prince, W. F. 1933. The case against Margery. *Scientific American* 148:261–63.

Randi, J. 1982. *Flim-flam! Psychics, ESP, unicorns and other delusions*. Amherst, NY: Prometheus Books.

———. 1985. The role of conjurers in psi research. In *A Skeptic's Handbook of Parapsychology*, ed. P. Kurtz. Amherst, NY: Prometheus Books.

———. 1997. *An encyclopedia of claims, frauds, and hoaxes of the occult and supernatural*. New York: St. Martin's Griffin.

Rhine, J. B., and L. E. Rhine. 1927. One evening's observation on the Margery mediumship. *Journal of Abnormal and Social Psychology* 21:401–27.

Riniolo, T. C. 1994. Publication bias: A computer-assisted demonstration of excluding nonsignificant results from research interpretation. *Teaching of Psychology* 24:280–83.

———. 1999. Using a large control group for statistical comparison: evaluation of a between-groups median test. *Journal of Experimental Education* 68:75–88.

———. 2002. The attorney and the shrink: Clarence Darrow, Sigmund Freud, and the Leopold and Loeb trial. *Skeptic* 9:80–83.

Riniolo, T. C., M. Koledin, G. M. Drakulic, and R. A. Payne. 2003. An archival study of eyewitness memory of the *Titanic*'s final plunge. *Journal of General Psychology* 130:89–95.

Riniolo, T. C., and L. Nisbet. 2007. The myth of consistent skepticism: The cautionary case of Albert Einstein. *Skeptical Inquirer* 31:49-53.

Riniolo, T. C., and S. W. Porges. 1997. Inferential and descriptive influences on measures of respiratory sinus arrhythmia: Sampling rate, R-wave trigger accuracy, and variance estimates. *Psychophysiology* 34:613–21.

Riniolo, T. C., and S. W. Porges. 2000. Evaluating group distributional characteristics: Why psychophysiologists should be interested in qualitative departures from the normal distribution. *Psychophysiology* 37:21–28.

Riniolo, T. C., and L. A. Schmidt. 1999. Demonstrating the gambler's fallacy in an introductory statistics class. *Teaching of Psychology* 26:198–200.

———. 1999a. Testing psi and psi-missing: Do skeptics negatively influence ESP experiments? *Skeptic* 7:74–76.

———. 2000. Searching for reliable relationships with statistics packages: An empirical example of the potential problems. *Journal of Psychology* 134:143–51.

———. 2006. Chronic heat stress and cognitive development: An example of thermal conditions influencing human development. *Developmental Review* 26:277–90.

Riniolo, T. C., and L. I. Torrez. 2000. Revisiting the monkey trial: Mr. Bryan's cross-examination of the defense. A speculative case study in the relationship of science and religion. *Skeptic* 8:60–63.

Riniolo, T. C., and M. Yerger. In press. "Overlooked" sources of bias: A cautionary note. In *Developmental Psychophysiology*, ed. L. A. Schmidt and S. J. Segalowitz. New York: Cambridge University Press.

Romanes, G. J. 1883. *Animal intelligence.* London: Routledge & Kegan Paul.

Rosengren, K. S., and A. K. Hickling. 2000. Metamorphosis and magic: The development of children's thinking about possible events and plausible mechanisms. In *Imagining the Impossible: Magical, Scientific, and Religious Thinking in Children*, ed. K. S. Rosengren, C. N. Johnson, and P. L. Harris, 75–98. Cambridge: Cambridge University Press.

Rosengren, K. S., C. W. Kalish, A. K. Hickling, and S. A. Gelman. 1994. Exploring the relation between preschool children's magical beliefs and causal thinking. *British Journal of Developmental Psychology* 12:69–82.

Rothbart, M., and P. Birrell. 1977. Attitude and perception of faces. *Journal of Research in Personality* 11:209–15.

Russell, B. 1938. *Skeptical essays.* New York: W.W. Norton and Company.

Sagan, C. 1996. *The demon-haunted world: Science as a candle in the dark.* New York: Random House.

Schultz, D. P., and S. E. Schultz. 2004. *A history of modern psychology.* 8th ed. Belmont, CA: Wadsworth.

Schulz-Hardt, S., D. Frey, C. Lüthgens, and S. Moscovici. 2000. Biased information search in group decision making. *Journal of Personality and Social Psychology* 78:655–69.

Scopes, J. T. 1997. *The world's most famous court trial: Tennessee evolution case.* Union, NJ: Lawbook Exchange. (Original published in 1925 by National Book Company.)

Seckel, A. 2000. *The art of optical illusions.* Carlton Books.

Sheehy, G. 1976. *Passages: Predictable crises of adult life.* 1st ed. New York: Dutton.

Shermer, M. 2001. *Why people believe weird things: Pseudoscience, superstition, and other confusions of our time.* New York: Owl Books.

Simon, J. L. 1981. *The ultimate resource.* Princeton, NJ: Princeton University Press.

———. 1990. *Population matters: People, resources, environment, and immigration.* New Brunswick, NJ: Transaction Publishers.

———. 1993. *Good mood: The new psychology of overcoming depression.* Chicago: Open Court Publishing Company.

———. 1995. What does the future hold? The forecast in a nutshell. In *The State of Humanity*, ed. J. L. Simon, 642–60. Cambridge, MA: Blackwell Publishers.

———. 1999. *Hoodwinking the nation.* New Brunswick, NJ: Transaction Publishers.

Slusher, M. P., and C. A. Anderson. 1987. When reality monitoring fails: The role of imagination in stereotype maintenance. *Journal of Personality and Social Psychology* 52:653–62.

Sowell, T. 1995. *The vision of the anointed: Self-congratulation as a basis for social policy.* New York: Basic Books.

———. 1996. *Knowledge and decisions.* New York: Basic Books.

———. 1996a. *Migrations and cultures: A world view.* New York: Basic Books.

———. 2001. *The Einstein syndrome: Bright children who talk late.* New York: Basic Books.

———. 2002. *A conflict of visions: ideological origins of political struggles.* New York: Basic Books.

———. 2002a. *The quest for cosmic justice.* New York: Touchstone.

———. 2004. *Applied economics: Thinking beyond stage one.* New York: Basic Books.

———. 2004a. *Basic economics: A citizen's guide to the economy.* Rev. and expanded ed. New York: Basic Books.

Spanos, N. 1994. Multiple identity enactments and multiple personality disorder: A sociocognitive perspective. *Psychological Bulletin* 116:143–65.

Spencer, R. W., and J. R. Christy. 1990. Precise monitoring of global temperature trends from satellites. *Science* 268:59–68.

Stossel, J. 2004. *Give me a break.* New York: HarperCollins Publishers.

Subbotsky, E. 2000. Phenomenalistic perception and rational understanding in the mind of an individual. In *Imagining the Impossible: Magical, Scientific, and Religious Thinking in Children,* ed. K. S. Rosengren, C. N. Johnson, and P. L. Harris, 35–74. Cambridge: Cambridge University Press.

Swann, W. B., Jr. 1997. The trouble with change: Self-verification and allegiance to the self. *Psychological Science* 8:177–80.

Tetlock, P. E. 1998. Close-call counterfactuals and belief-system defenses: I was not almost wrong but I was almost right. *Journal of Personality and Social Psychology* 75:639–52.

———. 1999. Theory-driven reasoning about plausible pasts and probable futures in world politics: Are we prisoners of our preconceptions? *American Journal of Political Science* 43:335–66.

Thagard, P. 1998. Ulcers and bacteria I: Discovery and acceptance. *Studies in History and Philosophy of Biological and Biomedical Studies* 9:107–36.

Thompson, D. W. J., and S. Solomon. 2002. Interpretation of recent Southern Hemisphere climate change. *Science* 296:895–99.

Thompson, L. G., E. Mosley-Thompson, M. E. Davis, K. A. Henderson, H. H. Brecher, V. S. Zagorodnov, T. A. Mashiotta, P.-N. Lin, V. N. Mikhalenka, D. R. Hardy, and J. Beer. 2002. Kilimanjaro ice core records: Evidence of Holocene climate change in tropical Africa. *Science* 298:589–93.

Tietze, T. R. 1972. *Margery.* New York: Harper & Row.

Trolier, T. K., and D. L. Hamilton. 1986. Variables influencing judgments of correlational relations. *Journal of Personality and Social Psychology* 50:879–88.

True, R. M. 1949. Experimental control in hypnotic age regression states. *Science* 110:583–84.

Vyas, N. K., M. K. Dash, S. M. Bhandari, N. Khare, A. Mitra, and P. C. Pandey. 2003. On the secular trends in sea ice extend over the Antarctic region based on OCEANSAT-1 MSMR observations. *International Journal of Remote Sensing* 24:2277–87.

Wager, T. D., J. K. Rilling, E. E. Smith, A. Sokolik, K. L. Casey, R. J. Davidson, S. M. Kosslyn, R. M. Rose, and J. D. Cohen. 2004. Placebo-induced changes in fMRI in the anticipation and experience of pain. *Science* 303:1162–67.

Walsh, J. 1996. *Unraveling Piltdown: The science fraud of the century and its solution.* New York: Random House.

Wason, P. C. 1960. On the failure to eliminate hypotheses in a conceptual task. *Quarterly Journal of Experimental Psychology* 12:129–40.

Watson, J. B., and R. Rayner. 1920. Conditioned emotional reactions. *Journal of Experimental Psychology* 3:1–14.

Watters, E., and R. Ofshe. 1999. *Therapy's delusions: The myth of the unconscious and the exploitation of today's walking worried.* New York: Scribner.

Weiner, J. S. 1955/2003. *The Piltdown forgery.* Oxford: Oxford University Press.

Wheeler, D. L., J. W. Jacobson, R. A. Paglieri, and A. A. Schwartz. 1993. An experimental assessment of facilitated communication. *Mental Retardation* 31:49–60.

Wilcox, R. R. 1998. How many discoveries have been lost by ignoring modern statistical methods? *American Psychologist* 53:300–14.

Wood, R. W. 1904. The n-rays. *Nature* 70:530–31.

Wood, W. J. 1912. Construction of the *Titanic. Marine Review* 11:160–64.

Woolley, J. D., K. E. Phelps, D. L. Davis, and D. J. Mandell. 1999. Where theories of mind meet magic: The development of children's beliefs about wishing. *Child Development* 70:571–87.

Zimmerman, P. R., J. P. Greenberg, S. O. Wandiga, and P. J. Crutzen. 1982. Termites: A potentially large source of atmospheric methane, carbon dioxide, and molecular hydrogen. *Science* 218:563–65.

INDEX